Book Reviews

"Lorna Faith knows how doubts can sabotage one's ability to write. In fact, this book addresses this, and how one could overcome those doubts and finally write that book you've always dreamt of writing.

Through examples from her own painful experiences, she shares specific steps through a proven formula that will enable struggling writers to overcome their own doubts and negative mindsets to begin creating again. I've read many books on writing, but I've never come across one presented in such a compassionate way as this one.

It exudes hope, wisdom, and full of practical exercises to help writers finally breakthrough whatever barriers they've been struggling with to write, at last, the book they were destined for."
Carrie ~ Amazon Reviewer

Finish Your Book

7 Steps to Unlock Your Creativity and Accelerate Your Writing Goals

Lorna Faith

"There is no greater agony than bearing an untold story inside you." Maya Angelou ~ *I Know Why the Caged Bird Sings*

Introduction

"...the one thing that you have that nobody else has is you. Your voice, your mind, your story, your vision. So write and draw and build and play and dance and live as only you can.
The moment you feel that, just possibly, you're walking down the street naked, exposing too much of your heart and your mind and what exists on the inside, showing too much of yourself. That's the moment you may be starting to get it right."
Neil Gaiman,
Commencement Speech 2012, University of the Arts

"What's wrong with me?" Tears ran down my cheeks as I blurted out my frustrations to my husband.

"I start a novel I'm all excited to write, but then about a third of the way into the story, I'm stuck. It seems with almost every book I write, I have this huge struggle with fear to finish it and I don't know why!"

Introduction

I was in the beginning chapters of Book Two in my Historical Romance series at the time. I was so discouraged, because even after I wrote a detailed ten page outline - for which I'd paid an editor to give me advice on where I could make changes - I still struggled to finish this book.

Which meant I was desperate to understand what hindered my writing. I panicked at the thought of staying stuck, especially when this was a story I was passionate to write and I had the outline right in front of me.

Questions plagued me. Was I just that bad of a writer that I couldn't pull the story together? Was I lazy? Was I not smart enough to figure out how to write stories? This particular day it seemed like all my doubts, worries and fears had set up an ambush and pounced on any confidence I had left.

"First of all, there's nothing wrong with you." Murray replied softly.

As usual, his words were the voice of reason bringing calm to my troubled world. He gave me a hug, doing his best to quiet my fears.

"And before you even ask, you are not lazy or too dumb to learn how to figure this out either."

I offered a small smile and sighed. He knew me well.

"Then, what am I missing?"

Introduction

"I'm not sure, but I do know this: you need to keep at it." He paused his hands on my shoulders, his eyes searching mine for courage that at the moment had slithered away into hiding. "Right now you need to grab hold of that dog-on-a-bone determination of yours and commit to keep writing and learning and then writing some more so you can figure that out."

His words were like a peak at the sun after a raging storm - they not only calmed my inner turmoil but sparked a new resolve to figure out what was holding me back in my writing journey.

So I started. I began to read more books, in an effort to learn more about what was holding back my creativity.

It was right around that time, I picked up Julia Cameron's amazing book on unblocking your creativity, *The Artist's Way*.

I also read Brene Brown's books: *Daring Greatly* and *The Gifts of Imperfection* and learned how to bravely let myself be vulnerable and to develop self-compassion. Then only a few months later I read Elizabeth Gilbert's helpful book on learning to be brave: *Big Magic: Creative Living Beyond Fear*.

Coincidence? I don't think so. This seemed more like a Divine nudge to begin to explore my own creativity and dive deeper into learning what held back my writing.

Introduction

I began to learn.

I started by making a commitment to write those three handwritten *Morning Pages* everyday as encouraged by Julia Cameron.

I learned that a big part of what hindered my writing process was a lack of self-compassion for mistakes and failures.

I learned how to be gentle on myself and to give myself permission to embrace the wonder - and the mistakes - which are a natural part of every writer's process.

I finally finished Book Two in that Historical Romance series in March 2016.

But, as happy as I was to finally have finished that book, the real reward was the awareness that little by little I was starting to write with more freedom.

As I continued my learning curve, I soon realized that perfectionism - and her twin sister procrastination - were both a very real hindrance to my writing.

As I began to write my next historical romance, I continued to learn how to unblock from those fears that held me back for so long. Along the way I have self-published another historical romance, a short novella, this nonfiction book and two romance novels under a pen name.

Introduction

As of this writing, I am happily growing into a steady rhythm with writing and self-publishing my books. I'm not a fast writer(not yet anyway), but my writing has accelerated in proportion to the new creative freedom I've uncovered as I've committed to practice these 7 steps I share in the following chapters.

Because of what seemed like an impossible journey of learning to write, self-publish and market books, a passion began to grow in me to help other writers.

If you struggle to write and finish your book, come join me and other writers over at CreateAStoryYouLove.com.

I've been blogging there since 2016 and have also had the privilege of interviewing many successful Indie Authors on the podcast. The podcast is on a pause for right now to make more space for writing, but I continue to write blogposts and create YouTube videos to help writers.

These days I am more excited than I've ever been to write the stories I'm passionate about.

In this struggle to finish my own books, I've come to a new realization that life really is too short to spend all your time writing stories you don't love.

Write those books that you are passionate about. Write a story that touches you as well as your readers' hearts.

Get clarity on the heart of why you want to write and commit to do whatever you need to do to uncover and unblock from whatever hindrances are holding you back from reaching your writing dreams.

One of my biggest lessons learned from finishing my own books is...

If you will commit to regular focused practice of learning: a successful author mindset, the craft of writing, compassionate creative unblocking and finding your writing rhythm, you will soon see a shift into greater joy, freedom and acceleration in your writing.

Just a little update: As of summer 2022, I have also written 8 sweet romance books under a pen name and now earn four figures a month with those books.

Through trial and error, and struggle to finish my books, I have continued to write and finish books that I'm passionate to write.

You can write and finish your book too!

Whether you're at the beginning stages of writing your first book, or if you've written a few books but still struggle to finish them, I hope the seven simple steps in this book help you unlock your writing dreams.

A Bird's Eye View of this book

Chapter One covers how to develop a clear vision for why you write. This is about deciding the reason why you need to write your book(s) and choosing to let your passion and commitment carry you through the obstacles on your writing path.

Introduction

Chapter Two steps into how to clear your creative path in three key areas that hinder you from writing and finishing your book.

Chapter Three moves into learning six simple steps to help you calculate your strategy for writing and finishing your book.

Chapter Four is about reminding yourself of your compelling reason to write your book and learning what it means to count the cost and commit to finishing it.

Chapter Five moves into discovering how to rewire and refocus your creative mind so that you can concentrate on reaching your goals.

Chapter Six is about how to charge up and level up in your writing practice to help you be fully present, push past obstacles and passionately create your own journey as a writer.

Chapter Seven covers simple steps on how you can converge into your new normal. Discover how to continue to close the gap between where you are and where you want to be in your writing and how to use self-compassion to give you greater freedom to get there.

You can go directly to the chapter you're interested in reading, or you can read the book in order. There are helpful questions, books and resources listed throughout the book, and if you like, you can download the list at this link at:

https://www.createastoryyoulove.com/ finishyourbookdownload

Please note: This book has some affiliate links to products or services that I recommend and enjoy using myself. This means that if you purchase through my links, I receive a small percentage of the sale, at no extra cost to you.

Chapter One

Clarify Your Reason For Writing

S TART AT THE VERY BEGINNING

"This I believe, is the central question upon which all creative living hinges: Do you have the courage to bring forth the treasures that are hidden within you?"
    Elizabeth Gilbert, Big Magic

So how do you go about getting clarity on your reason for writing your book? How do you find the gems that are hidden inside of you?

You need to start at the very beginning, much like you did when you were a small child.

Remember how as a kid you played and innocently

followed what piqued your interests? As you take a playful approach like you did as a child and follow naturally where your curiosity, wonder and excitement takes you, you'll uncover more of your passions.

Small children just let their curiosity lead the way and that's how they discover what makes them happy, sad, or what is exciting or interesting to them. They are organically led to that which creates wonder and passion inside them.

Let that be your guide too.

I realize that's easier said than done. The truth is, many times as adults we have learned through the school of hard knocks that we will face rejection, criticism or failure when we take a risk and begin those things we are passionate about doing.

So, because of the painful wounds and disappointments from our past, we've learned to be afraid to embrace our dreams.

We've learned to hold back and procrastinate on stepping out into the unknown to follow our curiosity.

We've learned to stay safe and instead shy away from digging too deeply inside ourselves to find those nuggets of gold that are surely there.

We've learned that anything more than staying in our comfortable, safe and predictable jobs and day-to-day familiar patterns, will cause us disappointment and pain.

So instead, we choose to play it safe and not take the risk, because anything else is much too scary.

The Mind Games that Fear Plays

I know the mind games fear can play, because I grew up afraid of so many things.

Growing up on a farm as the youngest of eleven children gave me a lot of fear-inducing moments. I watched helplessly as my sister fell down from a fifteen foot tree-fort(she couldn't breathe for awhile and I thought she was dead).

I fell through the ice in the creek while skating, the bull chased me when I would get the cows from the far pasture, I got zapped by the electric fence more than once, I nearly got ran over by a car and the list of scary things goes on and on.

Out of all those fears however, nothing was quite as devastating as being excited to tell stories and then hearing those awful words from my teacher that my writing was like chicken scratchings.

Because I was taught to respect my teacher and believed his words to be true, I stopped writing for over twenty years. It wasn't until I started homeschooling our four children and teaching them to write stories, that the passion and dream for storytelling came back to me once again.

All those years later, I began writing in a little notebook, secretly for a while, afraid of my own dream. But once I started, I couldn't help but continue to scribble in my little notebook whenever an idea would bubble up about a story.

My dream for writing stories grew until finally I got serious about writing my first novel. It was a big learning curve to glean from other authors how to self-publish my book, but I finally got the book out into the world.

The point in sharing that story of my own fears is to hopefully help you see the very humanness and normalcy of fear but that we don't have to let fear make decisions for our lives.

Learn to put fear in its place

People everywhere have to deal with different triggers of fears. I've learned that our response or reaction to fears should be different depending on the type of fears we're dealing with.

This is where we learn to put fear in its place.

If your fear is based on survival, then this is a necessary and healthy type of fear. If you didn't have some kind of fear to stop you from walking into oncoming traffic, most likely your life would be tragically cut short. So those types of fears are helpful.

However, if your fear tends to show up when you have innovative ideas and you step into creativity that has an unknown outcome, this is the bad kind of fear that wants to talk you out of following your natural curiosity.

When that fear shows up in a last ditch effort to stop you from stepping out and following those ideas that spark your curiosity, your response to fear is likely one of two things: *You either agree with the fearful thoughts as they enter your mind, or you allow yourself to feel the fear but choose to tell the fear that it's no longer in charge.*

At the most basic level, you will always feel some sort of fear when trying something new.

The important thing to remember is not to let fear make your decisions for you.

Instead, let that spark of curiosity and passion guide you, while still giving a head nod to risks involved in the decisions you make.

Here's the thing: anytime you want to do something that has the potential for greater positive impact in the lives of others, you will face resistance.

Steven Pressfield in his helpful book, *The War of Art*, helps put fear in perspective for anyone brave enough to risk following their passion. He says:

"Are you paralyzed with fear? That's a good sign. Fear is good. Like self-doubt, fear is an indicator. Fear tells us what we have to do. Remember our rule of thumb: The more scared we are of a work or calling, the more sure we can be that we have to do it." Steven Pressfield

Choose to be the artist who feels the fear and follows her heart anyway.

Choose to be the artist who feels self-doubt and writes her story anyway.

Choose to be the artist who experiences resistance and explores hidden depths inside herself anyway.

If you're paralyzed by fear, you know what you have to do.

Do the work afraid, but get it done.

Write your book and finish it. Whether it is the novel you've been itching to write, the nonfiction book that will inspire or help others, or the memoir that is important to the growth of your soul.

Begin today.

You'll be so glad you did.

. . .

Three essential ingredients needed to help you finish your book

One thing I've noticed as I've continued to write, is that there is more than one ingredient that is needed to help finish your book.

It's not enough to tell yourself that you'll finish your book.

For most writers, it takes more than the willingness to power through it to actually do the difficult job of writing and finishing their book.

For instance, if I lack a **clear vision** for the overall book, I won't have a clear strategy to hit the target.

If I lack **passion** for the book I'm writing, whether it's fiction or nonfiction, that lack of passion will stop the flow of work and cause me to stay stuck, unable to finish.

If I lack **commitment** to simply sit down and write consistently, the hard part of putting words on the blank page won't get done.

Clarity of Vision

A vague idea to write your book once in awhile, will make finishing it haphazard at best. I know this from personal experience.

When I wrote my first novel, I didn't start with any sort of plan, other than that I wanted to write a historical romance.

So, I simply started writing. I didn't begin with any

sort of idea of where I was going or any plan for when the novel should be done.

I didn't really have clarity on what my novel was about or when I wanted it to be finished.

The result was that this novel took the longest to write. It took me a little more than five years to finish that first book.

This is why it's so important to get a clear vision for your book.

Asking yourself questions is another really great way to bring clarity to your vision.

Here is a sample of some of the questions I ask when I have an idea for a book:

• **Who am I?**(are you a nurturer who cares for people; a fun person who loves socializing all day; or are you someone who loves being by themselves - an analytical data person who loves numbers).

• **What are some universal themes in my life that make me relatable to my readers?** (some examples of this are the pain of love; good vs. evil; loss of innocence).

• **What are the stakes I'm facing?**(maybe you promised yourself that you would finish this book and if you don't you know you'll regret it later). What are my fears or limiting beliefs?(Maybe you have self-doubt or fear of rejection and failure).

• **How have I sabotaged or self-sacrificed in my life?**(maybe at some point you had to sacrifice your dream of writing to take care of your family for awhile).

• **What was the resistance I faced?**(maybe

you've experienced perfectionism, procrastination or feeling overwhelmed).

• **What was the first shift that caused me to pivot in a new direction?**(maybe a friend encouraged you to start your book or a sudden job loss caused you to rethink what you are doing).

• **What are two options that were in front of me?**(maybe your options were to go back to school, or write your book).

• **Why did I choose the path I chose?**(maybe you felt that if you didn't write your book now, you wouldn't get another chance).

Asking and answering these kinds of questions really helps us to discover our why and the passion behind why we are writing the books we do.

Next, you can narrow down your questions to make them more specific about your book:

• **Why am I passionate to write this specific book?**

• **What are stories I've read or themes in my own life that really resonate with me?**

• **What are stories I've read and themes that I relate to?**

• **How does this book fit into my overall long-term plan as an author?**

One of the best ways to get really clear on your goals and vision, is to write out your mission statement as an author.

What is a mission statement?

A mission statement is a brief description of an individual or company's purpose. It sets out the goals, purpose and work of a person or organization. A mission statement clearly defines your values, ethics and fundamental goals.

When I was trying to get clear on my own mission statement as an author, it took me a few drafts to get it to where I thought this said what I wanted it to say.

I walk you through my mission statement below. Maybe it'll help you as you write your own.

I want to use my life experiences, my love of adventure and life to create compelling stories and characters to inspire hope, happiness and love and help readers feel in new and deeper ways.

I want to be continually learning new ways to improve my storytelling craft with every new fiction or nonfiction book I write.

My goal is to create a body of work that reaches many readers. I'm motivated to help many new writers to have their own "aha" moments that they really can have a fresh start, that they can begin again, that they can write the books they love and make money with their writing.

I usually tweak this mission statement a little every year as I grow and learn about myself, my passions and how those passions intersect with what helps others in their struggles to write their stories.

The process of writing a mission statement helps you develop a deep understanding of the reasons you are writing. This understanding is critical to your focus, clarity and motivation as a writer.

It's important to know why you are passionate to write your book because it will help you stay committed to a regular writing practice so you can finish your book.

Listed below, are a few reasons people write their books. Maybe one or two will resonate with you:

- You want to write compelling novels with memorable characters and storylines to entertain and inspire readers.
- You have gone through a life changing experience and you want to help others who are going through the same thing.
- You have an insatiable curiosity about a particular subject and you want to write about it.
- You want to write a book on a specific topic that will help you work out what you think along with helping others who are interested in the same topic.
- You want to build your authority and credibility in a specific niche or industry.
- You want to write nonfiction books that are centred around a specific niche so you can dominate the market in that niche resulting in book sales becoming a steady source of income.
- You want to write fiction books and series of fiction books in a genre to attract readers interested in that genre to create a steady source of income from your fiction books.
- You already have an audience of readers/listeners (blog, podcast, YouTube), and you want to write books to satisfy what they want to learn from you and at the same time write what interests you.
- You want to leave a legacy.

When you really understand your personal reasons for

writing your book, it will help you move forward at an accelerated pace.

In the end, this will save you time because you'll be so clear on who you are and what you offer to the world.

When you are clear on your vision, you won't climb the wrong mountain.

Clarity of Passion

Another important piece of the puzzle is clarity of passion. While it's great to ask yourself a bunch of questions to narrow down your vision for writing, it's also important to get clear on why you are passionate about something.

Here's an important part of discovering and getting clarity of passion. You can't just think your way toward finding your passion, you have to act your way to your truth, from the inside out.

I can only tell you this is true from my own experience.

For example, for years I wanted to write a book. I thought about it, but always would talk myself out of it, usually because of fears that held me back. Finally when I was homeschooling our four children, I mentioned it to my husband that I might like to try to write a novel.

He encouraged me to get started.

It wasn't until I put pen to paper and started writing that I realized how good it felt to write stories. Even though my own limiting beliefs kept trying to claw their way back into my subconscious and conscious mind, I continued to write just a little.

It was the action of describing my characters and putting words to the settings I saw in my mind's eye that felt so good.

Writing stories and coming up with words that matched the movie playing in my mind was an amazing feeling. It was freeing. It was wonderful.

I share this with you to encourage you to take action on your writing dream today.

By the simple act of writing for ten minutes on a book you've been thinking about for awhile, you'll discover that spark of passion.

It really is magical, when you begin to be actively engaged doing something you suspect might be your passion.

When you bring your full focus and attention to your writing, pouring your heart and soul into it like you really want to, you'll begin to see a shift toward more creativity and insight.

This shift to more creativity in that which you're really passionate to do, is something I've experienced on two levels: as a singer songwriter and also as writer of fiction and nonfiction.

I discovered as I wrote songs and poured my heart into them that it really resonated with the passion inside me, doing this resonated with more listeners. I've discovered this to also be true with writing.

But you have to be willing to be vulnerable and write your story.

You have to be willing to commit to a regular writing process.

. . .

Clarity of Commitment

As soon as we decide we're going to be committed to writing and finishing our book that seems to be when self-doubt, fear and other limiting beliefs show up to challenge our commitment.

Our rational mind taunts us with questions like: *I was never any good at writing, this won't work; What if I fail? What if nobody reads my book? What if my family and close friends mock what I'm doing and tell me I'm ruining my life by committing so much time to writing?*

If you've ever ask yourself any of the questions above, I want to tell you you're not alone.

All the writers I've interviewed and talked with struggle with self-doubt and fear in one or more areas of their writer's journey.

Self-doubt and fear have been some of my biggest struggles. The result has been many days and weeks of procrastination or other forms of self-sabotage that have caused me to lose what traction I might have gained.

It never fails, the moment you find what you love to write, that's when some form of resistance shows up to challenge your new found commitment to finish your book.

When you get to this place of resistance, fear and self-doubt creeps in and gnaws away at your self-confidence.

This is when we begin to judge our writing as good or not so good.

Doubt about ourselves and our writing is normal for writers, but don't let that stop you from writing your story.

In the past couple years as I've begun to write more

often and more consistently, I've realized how similar writing is to many other practices.

Below, I share a little about lessons learned from many years of vocal practice.

My Lessons Learned from Gruelling Vocal Practice

Writing is similar to learning to sing. You are learning to lay down track each time you practice and you are developing your own sound and rhythm as you continue to learn and progress.

I'd like to share with you my story of learning to sing and developing a regular practice to improve my singing.

I remember when I was around thirteen years old, I wanted to learn to sing better, so I started at the beginning and began learning.

My teacher told me to practice at least five days a week because my voice was squeaky and very often my tone was flat. I was discouraged that I didn't sound as good as many other singers I had heard, but I wanted to learn to sing so badly, that I decided I would try any type of practice if it meant I would improve.

I thought maybe, just maybe I would get better at singing.

I had lessons with this teacher for a couple of years before either of us saw any noticeable improvement. Finally I learned what it meant to sit on top of a note, and how to sing from my diaphragm instead of my chest voice.

Part of this process meant I had to do all sorts of weird and embarrassing exercises like lying down flat on the hard floor and sing, because when you sing in that position it ensures that you are singing from your diaphragm.

I would sing with my arms flailing over my knees as if I was trying to touch my toes. Again this was so my teacher could double check that I was using my head voice and breathing deeply using my diaphragm.

Gradually with practice I got better at singing. Then, I went away from home to a boarding school for the last two years of high school. There, I took singing lessons again and I was in a high school group that travelled to different cities and a trio that sang for special occasions.

A few years after I graduated, I had this idea that I'd like to learn more music - both voice and piano - and study at a university. I had recently been married, and my hubby agreed this would be a good step for me to continue to develop musically.

So we moved back near the city where he grew up and I was accepted into the Bachelor of Music program for both piano and voice, which meant I had a choice. I chose singing as my major because it was my passion.

I took weekly lessons where I not only was required to learn to sing in five different languages, but also had to go to a soundproof room in the basement area of the university to practice five days a week.

While in the practice room, my voice teacher said I needed to stand in the corner(this helps you hear your sound better) and sing for most of the hour of practice time.

She explained that I had a vocal break between my high B and high F sound and I needed to push past that vocal break so my voice could get to an even tone and a new freedom of sound.

It was so frustrating to sing the same musical phrases over and over, often ten times in a row. I learned quickly that wherever I experienced a problem in vocal tone, language, or where my voice cracked, I needed to do a lot of practice.

I remember arriving at the weekly Voice MasterClass which included all the singing students, hoping against hope that my voice teacher wouldn't call my name because I feared the criticism and rejection.

I didn't want to hear about all the things I was doing wrong yet again.

Many times I went home after those classes and just cried because I was so frustrated with my voice, frustrated with myself and frustrated with all the criticism from my teacher and my peers(even though I knew they were right).

I was scared I wouldn't ever get any better at singing.

The good news was that after those first two years of really intense vocal practice, I was able to push through that vocal break to sing with a new clarity and freedom of sound.

All this practice I learned later, had also increased my vocal range to three and a half octaves. Some of the perks were that I was accepted into the University Singers choral group and asked to sing solos, including some of my favourite arias and spirituals, for different concerts in the area.

All those years of regular practice helped shift my mindset and helped me finally get that breakthrough in my voice.

Those years of committed practice, taught me the great value of persistence and repetition in learning to get better at something.

Develop a Mindset of Practice

Some lessons learned through this process is what I had applied to the practice of singing could be applied to other skills as well.

So, when the spark to write stories came back again, I realized I could apply the same principles and overall strategy to help me write better.

You can too.

I want to encourage you that no matter where you are in your writing journey, you can learn to develop a mindset of practice.

Think back to your childhood for a moment. Was there anything you did that required regular practice? This could be something like learning to play a sport, learning to play an instrument or learning to ride a bike.

Do you remember the regular practice that was needed for you to get better at that skill?

Here's what I've learned. Whenever there is a new skill you are passionate to learn, developing a mindset of practice is a necessity to continue to get better at it.

Remember, that no matter how awful you feel your writing is right now or how much you feel like your writing is filled with holes, cracks and rejection, just know that with regular practice you can and will get better at writing.

Granted, sometimes the constant writing practice will

feel gruelling and you might cry with frustration and want to quit like I did with singing(and with writing if truth be told).

However, as much as you might want to quit, I encourage you to stick with it. Keep writing. You don't have to write perfectly, you just need to keep at it.

This idea of focusing on the process and what you're learning instead of focusing on the end product is something that Thomas Sterner talks about in an interview I had with him on the topic of developing a Practicing Mind(link in the resources at the end of the chapter).

He shares steps on how you can train your mind to enjoy what you're creating in the present moment so you can be fully engaged.

To be able to stick to a consistent writing practice, you need to keep your reasons why you write in front of you every day.

Write down the reason you are compelled to write this book. Put it by your writing desk. Write it on a sticky note that you put on your bathroom mirror. Stick it somewhere where you'll see it and be reminded of it every day.

Remember, the reason you want to write doesn't have to be world changing.

Your reason for writing simply needs to be personal to you. Your big why just needs to resonate deeply inside of you. Your reason for writing needs to be necessary for you.

When you clarify your reasons for writing your book and it resonates deeply inside of you, then you will feel the motivation and inspiration to begin.

The passion you have to write will loom large in your

mind, sticking to you like glue and you'll be excited to finish your book.

Something to try...

At the end of each chapter, I try offer some simple steps for you to begin to put into practice what you've learned.

I encourage you to take a few minutes to answer the questions below and to check out the helpful resources.

I believe that going through these exercises will help bring the clarity and inspiration to finish your book.

Questions to ask yourself:

What is your compelling reason to write and finish your book?

• What are 3 obstacles or fears you have about finishing your book? How can you step past those fears and engage your passion?

• What is your mission statement as a writer? Do your best to answer questions like: *Who are you? What stories resonate and inspire you?*

• What are some universal themes you see in your own life? Some examples: *going broke; divorce; losing someone or something.* Which of those themes(or other themes) do you feel drawn to write?

• What skill have you learned in life, where you had to learn regular practice? How can you apply that to writing and finishing your book?

. . .

Resources to help you:

• If you feel you need to re-ignite your passion for writing your story, I encourage you to read the blogpost below: https://www.createastoryyoulove.com/7-ways-to-reignite-your-passion-for-writing/

• How to develop a Practice Mind to go into laser focus with your writing. Interview with Thomas Sterner: www.createastoryyoulove.com/thomassterner

• *Big Magic: Creative Living Beyond Fear* by Elizabeth Gilbert

• *The War of Art: Break Through The Blocks and Win Your Inner Creative Battles* by Steven Pressfield

Chapter Two

Clear Your Path

*"I deal with writer's block by lowering my expectations.
I think the trouble starts when you sit down to write and
imagine that you will achieve something magical and
magnificent—and when you don't, panic sets in.*

*The solution is never to sit down and imagine that you will
achieve something magical and magnificent.
I write a little bit, almost every day, and if it results in two
or three or (on a good day) four good paragraphs, I consider
myself a lucky man.
Never try to be the hare. All hail the tortoise."*
Malcolm Gladwell

Have you ever sat down to write, only to be distracted, to procrastinate or have a head-on collision with some other form of resistance?

If you've experienced any of the above, I can only say welcome to a writer's everyday world.

I've struggled with a love / fear relationship with every book I sit down to write. It's not surprising then, that countless times that I've just sat down to write, I've decided I need to get up to get a drink of water or have a disturbing need to check email or social media.

What ends up happening - after I berate myself - is that the days, weeks and sometimes months have gone by without any words on the page to show for it.

For years I asked myself over and over again what is wrong with me that I have this continual self-defeating pattern. Much later, I finally realized that I needed to unblock writing roadblocks, so that I could write with greater freedom.

What happens when you continue to have this pattern of not achieving the goals you set for yourself, is that you begin to fear that you'll never live up to your full potential. You start to feel like you're a fraud or an imposter who isn't worthy of success. You start to believe there's no hope that you will ever achieve your writing dreams.

When we start to believe that, many of us find ways to distract ourselves by doing things like cleaning the house, doing the dishes or keeping our schedules so full that we don't have time to write. This is another way writers can procrastinate or delay our dreams.

. . .

Do you relate to any of the above hindrances to writing your book?

Are you ready to get to the root cause of this pattern of self-sabotage to unlock your writing dreams?

It's my hope that this chapter gives you helpful tips and strategy on how to clear your path so you can write.

I've learned in my own writing journey as I've coached other writers to finish their book, that it's nearly impossible to achieve your goals until you clear your path of obstacles, roadblocks and other hindrances.

So what are some hindrances that stand in our way that stop us from reaching our goals?

I've noticed that there are three areas that are big obstacles for many writers to finish their book. There are many more, but the big ones are the ones I will share with you below.

Why It's Important to Unblock Writing Roadblocks in 3 Key Areas

There are really three key areas that I've seen most writers struggle with challenges. These are areas that I've struggled with myself, and so I hope that reading through this will cause a paradigm shift in the way you see your author journey.

Getting rid of hindrances that try to trap us and keep us stuck is vital to tap into the creativity that each one of us has inside of us.

Unblocking your creative path is key to activating and implementing your goals as a writer.

In truth, without building a successful writing mind-set, it's often impossible to get any forward motion with writing or growing our author platform and reaching more readers.

A great question to dig deep and ask yourself is: *How do I go to a new level in my mindset so I can write and finish my book(s)?*

A helpful place to start is to look at the book(or books) you are currently writing as an opportunity to lead others. Understand the themes you are passionate about that keep coming up in your own life over and over again.

Then when you write, choose to let this theme naturally come up in your writing. This is true for nonfiction as you share your knowledge about topics you are passionate about, but I believe it also applies to writers of fiction.

I can tell you from my teen years to adult years, that the fiction authors whose books I read were people whom I saw as mentors.

You might be asking, how does looking at my writing as an opportunity to lead others, have to do with levelling up my mindset?

Good question. Here's what I've noticed in myself as well as other first-time writers. Many of our mindset challenges start because we are coming from a victim mentality around the roadblocks that are in our way.

But, our mindset doesn't have stay that way. We can be empowered to switch our mindset to break free of old habits to that of creating results.

. . .

Each of us has the ability to shift our mindset and step into that leadership role at any time in our writing journey.

How we see ourselves, people around us, and ideas that come to us, this is what surrounds our thoughts and environment everyday.

This is what feels normal to us everyday.

These thought patterns that we see as normal, is our everyday way of thinking that essentially has us operating on autopilot.

So, in order to create a new normal and shift out of habit patterns that limit us, we have to decide which thoughts are helping us and which are hindering us as we take steps toward our new and sometimes intimidating writing goals.

Since very often these habit patterns have been on autopilot for years, we have a difficult time seeing which thought patterns fall into the categories of normal and foreign for the goals we are trying to achieve.

One of the keys to make a shift and implement successful writing habits, is to work on mindset.

Thought patterns are different from what we've known in the past.

A good example of shifting from a 'normal' to 'foreign' habit pattern is if you've ever gone on a diet or have chosen to change your eating habits.

This is something I've done recently. I've decided to

make the switch to clean eating. It's not easy to change habits that you've had for years. You have to remind yourself everyday what you're doing and why you're doing it.

For myself, I wanted to get healthier. So I chose to eat salads, veggie meals and to get rid of the sugar, even though it's been a difficult and bumpy ride.

Even though I feel tons better with more energy and clear headedness throughout the day, it is still a choice I have to make everyday. Sometimes I fail in those choices, but I aim to choose healthy eating. I've needed to change my thought patterns around food and continually remind myself why I'm eating this way.

Changing to a new way of eating is similar to shifting your mindset to reach your writing goals. More than likely old familiar thought patterns and habits simply need some encouragement to change.

To discern our thoughts we need to question them. Ask yourself if how you currently view yourself and your writing is helping you reach your writing goals?

Maybe the book you are trying to finish right now is something you've believed will take years to write. But what if you could cut that time in half? For example, what if you figured out that you could get your 70,000 word book written in six months or even three months?

It is doable.

It's just a matter of shifting your mindset and then figuring out what it's going to take for you to write your book so you can get it done to reach your deadline.

Dig deep inside and ask if the thought and habit patterns you currently have are helping you. Any big shift you make in your life means you'll need to learn to adapt new ways of thinking which become new habits and that's how we reach our goals.

Mindset affects how we take action and solve problems.

Your mindset has got you to where you are right now, and since you want to get to a different situation and goal, you'll need to be willing to make a switch to a different mindset and new habits.

What we want to do is go from the past situation to the new situation — which for many writers is to write more books, have more readers and make more money with our writing.

It's super helpful to find writing mentors who have already reached goals similar to yours.

Rather than using the same patterns of thoughts, actions and problem solving strategies to try to get us to our new goals, it's important to look at people who are already where we want to be and adapt their patterns of successful thinking, action and problem-solving so we get similar results.

3 Key Areas that Writers Need to Unblock

Most writers I know struggle in three key areas of their writing journey.

These are familiar to me as they are the same three areas that I struggled with for such a long time as I was learning to write books.

The three areas of focus in this chapter are: lack of self-confidence; lack of money and lack of writing habits.

· · ·

1.Lack of Self-Confidence.

Let's start by writing out the dictionary definition to help us narrow down what self-confidence means:

Definition: full trust; self-reliance; assurance; reliability of a person; assurance; realistic confidence or belief in one's own judgment; ability; power.

It stands to reason then, that if self-confidence is a realistic confidence or belief in one's own judgment, then if you have a lack of self-confidence, you don't have much confidence or belief in yourself.

This feeling of self-doubt and lack of self-confidence is what I struggled with for years. It is also one of the big reasons why I spent years dabbling on my first novel before I ever self-published it. Maybe some part of that resonates with your own writing journey.

To help us dive deeper into understanding the area of lack of self-confidence, I've listed below some examples of statements I've said myself and that I've also heard from other writers.

A) *I don't think my writing is good enough.*

It is very normal to feel this way. In fact, most first-time writers feel like everything they write isn't good enough for people to read. I've even read stories of well-known authors saying that every time they sit down to write the next book, they wonder if they have what it takes to write it.

There are many reasons you might feel like your writing isn't good enough.

Maybe writing in school wasn't a good subject for you

and you didn't do well in class where you wrote essays. Or maybe you feel like you came from a different background and didn't have as many opportunities. Or maybe you had a parent, teacher or mentor who spoke negatively about your writing or any of your other creative gifts, and it made you stop writing and doing what gave you joy.

I get that. I've heard a few different versions as to why writers feel like what they write won't be good enough.

This is a natural part of your safety mechanism inside of you that wants to keep you safe. This part of you(psychologists call it the Ego), wants to keep you safe, to protect you and keep you comfortable.

When you feel like your writing isn't good enough to share with the world, that's basically letting that inner ego win. The ego is saying "what you feel is more important than the value you will add to the world by writing this book."

In an interview with Pamela Hodges, she shares how she faced a lot of resistance as an painter and writer. She says it's a daily battle and the resistance you fight is as big as your dream. She inspires creatives everywhere to stop listening to the voice of resistance and just start(to listen to this interview, you can find the link in the resources at the end of this chapter).

One simple way of working through this is to focus on the benefits instead of that which makes you feel afraid. Some examples of benefits might be: people are waiting for you to finish writing your book; you want to leave a legacy for your family; or you want to earn an income from writing your book(s).

For example, writing this book is beyond my comfort

zone and I feel a lot of self-doubt creeping in. I wonder whether any ideas in this book will actually help readers to break through and begin to take steps toward their writing dreams. Yet, I feel compelled to write this book. I've experienced a big shift in my own thinking as I worked through writing my own books, and I feel I need to share the lessons I have learned.

In your own writing, I want to encourage you to focus on the benefits you'll gain from writing and finishing your book. Doing so will help you to take the action steps each day to reach your goals.

B) *What if nobody wants to buy my book?*

Again, most writers I know feel this fear of rejection.

Most people have a deep-seated fear of rejection. We are hard-wired to seek the approval of others. So when we do something new, something risky, our minds bring up many questions intended to make us think, to protect us. As writers, one of the questions that comes up is whether anyone will like or want to buy our books.

The biggest way to overcome the fear of rejection is to give yourself permission to write the story you are truly passionate about anyway. What this does, is frees you from needing the approval and validation from anyone else about your writing.

Beyond writing what you love, listed below are a few more tips that I hope will help you to move beyond fear of rejection so you can write with freedom.

Step a little out of your comfort zone and ask for feedback from readers and from your editor.

I've found that after I've self-edited my book, and gotten feedback from a few beta readers and an editor, often it is my readers invaluable suggestions that make the book even better.

Do another read through and self-edit of your book. Sometimes it's helpful if your book isn't selling well to go back through your book and tweak it. Consider changing the cover of the book. Browse through books in a similar genre to yours, and look at the covers. Cover art makes the first impression with a potential reader. Readers recognize and are attracted to books in similar genres by the book cover.

Another tip is to keep notes of reader reviews. For example, if they are telling you they would like more depth to your main character or if they would like the story to be more fleshed out and to go deeper, take notes and see how you could reshape your book.

It's also important to keep inspirational writer affirmations near your writing desk like: "Yes, I can write!" "I write with passion!" "My words are impacting readers!" "I take my writing seriously and work hard at my craft!" "I give grace to myself and accept that perfection is not the goal, only that I courageously tell my story."

I have an alarm set on my iPad to go off every morning as a reminder to speak my writing affirmations out loud. It's a great way to start the day!

I really hope some of these ideas help give you the freedom to write the story you are truly passionate about and to have fun doing it.

. . .

C) *I don't want to read any negative reviews of my book.*

There are many reasons not to read negative reviews of your book, and probably just as many reasons to read them.

There are many differing opinions on whether writers should read their negative reviews or not.

I choose not to read a review of my book that is less than three stars. If reviews are lower than that, I'll usually ask someone I trust (my daughters or hubby) to read them. I ask them to let me know if there is any constructive criticism in the review that would help me write better books. Otherwise I don't want to hear things like "this was the worst book I've ever read."

You choose what works for you.

The truth is, it's never very fun to get negative feedback. Negative feedback can potentially suck your desire to write out of you(which isn't helpful when you want to write more books).

Here's something to remember about reviews. They aren't about you as a person. It's more specifically about how a certain reader connects or resonates(or doesn't) with your message and what you have to say.

Remember that your book is only a snapshot of your message and story and it's a reflection of who you were at the time you wrote that book. So those negative reviews aren't a part of you, they are just a reaction to what that specific reader feels right now about your book.

In some ways, when you see reviews from that perspective, it allows you to disconnect from that feedback.

At the end of the day, it is good and helpful to get feedback for your writing. You decide if you want to read negative reviews or if you'd rather have someone you trust doing that and only relaying back to you feedback that is constructive and useful to you.

D) Only a few people get lucky and make money with their writing. I need to be more realistic with my writing dreams.

This statement is really giving away your power to create the career you want and to reach your writing dreams.

When writers say this, they are really coming from a place of wanting to 'be picked' or to get permission from gatekeepers like publishers, agents or anyone in authority who would validate you as an author.

This was seriously where I was at for years. Which is why I waited so long to self-publish my first book. I didn't realize that when you are waiting to 'be picked' you are giving your power away. You are saying that you have no control over whether your career as an author is successful.

It's simply not true that you have to wait to be picked or that you have no control over your writing career. Sure there are some areas where we can't decide. For example, we can't decide if we're going to be on the New York Times bestsellers list, but we can do specific things that will give us a greater chance to reach that goal.

The great news is that if you choose to self-publish

your book and become an independent author, you have a great deal of control over so much of your book's process.

It's true that there are some authors who work really hard and don't get to the place they want, but as an indie author, you have a lot of control over your situation.

You can always build your skill set, gather new resources, try again or switch ideas on the books you write. There are always details you can tweak to help get you to where you want to go.

E) I want the recognition and money for my book right now.

This is really about wanting to skip the journey and the transformation that every writer goes through when they write and finish one or more books.

Writing a book is a journey. The fascinating part of writing a book is something you don't hear many writers talk about: *as much as you are going to work on your book, your book is also going to work on you to change and transform you.*

Maybe that's why books are so powerful both for the writer and for the reader. A lot of transformation happens inside you as a writer as you write your book.

For instance, some things you learn are what your core themes are - themes that you come back to over and over again; what time of day is best for you to write, and what type or genre of book you are most passionate to write.

These are all wonderful things to learn about yourself and it really does catapult your growth as a writer.

There are phases you go through to become skilful or to master something.

The first phase is the frustration of struggling to learn something you haven't done before.

Most people dread learning a whole lot of new things and many times it's slow going as we make a lot of mistakes because we're not good at it yet.

So in the very beginning, we make a lot of mistakes and sometimes it feels like everyone else is having fun but us. The key is to focus on pushing forward during this phase.

The second phase is the struggle of practice.

This is where you choose to commit. Why? Because if you don't commit to learning and growing your skills so you can progress toward your writing dream, you're going to give up. If you give up, you won't get what you want or need and you won't become who you need to be and you won't have or be able to do what you dream of doing.

Going through these phases doesn't feel comfortable, but you need to just concentrate and get it done. That way you'll make big inroads on your project and you'll write and finish more books.

Something that I find helpful when struggling with my own impatience is to say out loud what I'm grateful for in my writing journey.

Practice saying out loud what you're grateful for.

For example, try saying the following out loud:

• I'm working on my writing dreams right now(as opposed to "I want to reach my dreams or I want to be at this next stage already).

• I'm happy because I'm working on my writing dream every single day. Even though I'm not where I want to be yet, and I haven't hit all the goals I want to reach, I'm excited that I can work on my dreams... right now, today.

I hope you find that helpful and that you are encouraged to keep going with your writing dreams.

In conclusion, I want to mention an amazing tip on confidence for creatives that I learned from creative coach Mark McGuinness from a blogpost he wrote on his website lateralaction.com.

Mark shares about what he has learned from his twenty-one years of coaching creatives:

> *Forget confidence and tap into your enthusiasm. Confidence is all about you "do I feel confident?" But enthusiasm takes you out of yourself.*
>
> *When you feel enthusiastic about something, you want to work on it, so you feel energized. You want to share it with others, which is infectious.*

Enthusiasm for writing the story that's in you and focusing on what you love most about

it will make your story come alive to you and to your readers.

Next, we'll talk about the second key area that is a roadblock for many writers: *lack of money*.

2. Lack of Money.

The longer I've been around writers, the more I've discovered that there are many authors who have road-blocks when it comes to a lack of money.

I was no exception to this and it's only through contin-ually learning and trying new things that my mindset has shifted on this.

Since money is a tool we use to gain the resources we need for everyday life, we need enough of it to sustain our life and to continue to learn and grow the skills we need to do what we love... like writing.

I've noticed in myself and others, that sometimes our perceptions around money represent how we value ourselves. For example, if we fear we'll never have enough money, this could possibly stem from inner feelings of inadequacy, insecurity or failure in other areas of our life.

On the other hand, if you believe that you'll be able to find another way to earn more money, this could possibly stem from your inner belief that you can find a solution for what you need at any given time and everything is figure-out-able.

So, let's dive deeper into some specific areas on tips to overcome obstacles around lack of money.

· · ·

A) I don't have the money and resources I need to succeed at writing.

You might be on a tight budget and barely getting by with bills to pay, kids to feed, or parents to help take care of. Maybe you don't have a lot of support around you with family or friends, or maybe you have other pressing needs.

I understand from personal experience, feeling like: *I can't pay for an editor; I don't have money for professional book cover; It's not in my budget to pay for that writing, self-publishing or book marketing course, or whatever else I needed at the time.*

Remember, it's really important to keep your vision for why you're writing your book(or books) in front of you at all times. I've found that when I lose sight of that, that's also when I lose my motivation to do whatever it takes to uncover resources I need.

Again, this really goes back to valuing yourself. Remind yourself that writing this book is your dream and you are worth the investment.

There are ways to work around dealing with a tight budget.

I've made a list below of ideas of how I've uncovered extra money or went out and got the resources I needed. These ideas come from my own personal experience and ideas from other writers, so I hope you find one or two of these useful in your own situation.

Tips on how to uncover extra money from your current budget:

- **Look at all your household bills and see where you can cut back.** I realize this isn't very fun, but this is when it's important to keep your focus on your long-term writing goal. This will inspire and motivate you to cut corners where you need to in the short term.

For example, I remember looking at our car insurance bill one month and I thought there must be another company whose rates were less per month. So I searched around on Google, and found different companies that served our area.

Sure enough, we were able to decrease our insurance by $40 a month. This also worked for our monthly Internet service bill and phone bill and we also were able to lower interest rates on our credit card so we could pay it off faster. In total we managed to save a little over $160 dollars a month.

- **If you're driving a brand new vehicle with monthly payments, consider switching to a used vehicle that you buy with cash.** When you do this, you'll no longer have the monthly payments. This is something my husband and I started doing when we first got married, and it not only saves money per month, but brings peace of mind too.

- **Cut back how on much you spend on extras like coffee, going out to eat or going to movies.** Again, not fun to cut back on extras, but so worth it if it means you can move forward faster to reach your writing dreams. Consider limiting your eating out as a family to once a month and commit to a limited budget for extras like Starbucks and other coffee or fast food places.

Since I've chosen healthier eating, I've really noticed less money going out. I want to encourage you to try cutting back your spending habits on extras. You'll be amazed at how doing this can really help save on your monthly budget.

Tips on how to reach out for the resources and money you need:

• **Consider bartering for what you need.** For example, if you need an editor for the book you're writing and you don't have the money to pay them, ask around different writers groups on Facebook and see if there is someone willing to trade your editing for something you do well.

Maybe you are great at social media, at designing websites or book covers or maybe you've learned how to format an ebook on Vellum or Scrivener. Offer a swap. You might be surprised at how many editors will take you up on your offer.

• **Begin to learn a new skill that you could offer freelance work from your home or from anywhere you have Internet access.** Maybe in the above example, you said to yourself: *I don't have skills I could offer in exchange for editing(or something else)*. If that's true, then there are a few places where you can learn new skills at a relatively low cost.

One example is udemy.com where you can take courses on designing book covers, how to design websites, how to be great at email marketing and many other courses that teach you useful skills. Then when you've learned the skill, offer your services for the going rate on your website and also mention it in different writers groups you're a part of.

• **Another idea is to consider a part-time job that could earn you extra finances.** This way you could begin saving for an editor, a book cover designer or for that online course to help you gain momentum to reach your writing goals.

I hope you find the above tips useful to you and maybe it sparks some ideas on how you could find the money in your budget so you can get the resources you need to finish your book(s).

There are a few more specific tips to help you uncover roadblocks around lack of money that I wanted to mention below.

B) There's no money in writing books.

It's simply not true that there is no money in writing books.

The amount of royalty rate you receive will vary according to which route you choose for publishing your book.

If you go the traditional publishing route you only earn between 7% - 25% royalty per each book sold. However if you choose to be an independent author(indie author), the royalty rate(as of this writing) is 70% on digital retailers like Amazon if you price your book between the $2.99 to $9.99 price range.

There are many authors I know who choose to self-publish their books and are making good money as authors.

A key thing to remember is that it's vital to keep learning from successful indie authors. I do this by listening to podcasts and blogposts by successful authors, so I can learn writing, self-publishing and marketing tips from them.

As you continue to learn, you'll discover new ideas and strategies that other indie authors are doing to find success in their writing journey. This is something I continue to do. Whenever I need to drive somewhere, I listen to a new podcast episode and it really helps me stay focused on my own writing journey and I learn a ton of new ideas as well, which is really great.

Realize that there is money in this industry, but it takes a lot of creative thinking to figure out how to earn or access that money.

Over the years I've discovered that the trick to receiving more finances into your life is to have many different paths where money can flow into your life.

For instance, you could write fiction or nonfiction and you could also create online courses or offer coaching services. Many authors are doing this, and are finding that having a few different streams of income diversifies and increases the flow of money into their lives.

When I think of different streams of income, I'm reminded of what my mom used to say: *Don't put all your eggs in one basket.* Sound advice.

. . .

C) *The money doesn't matter or it is secondary as I write books.*

Maybe you have different financial resources available to you that keeps all your bills paid. If you are in this situation, then that's awesome and it should free you up to write.

However, if you tell yourself money doesn't matter then that really is another way of not valuing yourself. In our economy, money does matter and it's important to take care of your money and finances because that's what takes care of you. When you have the money situation more in hand, you're able to impact the world more.

The interesting thing about having impact, is that the more resources you have available to you, the further you're able to spread your message.

When we're doing our best to serve others, sometimes we can tell ourselves: *I just want to do this for free.* It is super helpful to offer a few things for free as you serve others, like the first book in a series(I've done that with this series of nonfiction books). But, if you gave everything away for free, then how would you support yourself and be able to continue to have an impact on others around you?

The more resources and finances you have at your fingertips, the more potential you have to impact others.

You can value yourself and bring value to others at the same time by getting your message into the world.

Continue to write your books and build resources that help others around you and become an abundant person in all aspects of your life.

. . .

3. Lack of Writing Habits.

Starting a regular writing habit was something I struggled with for years. I learned that my failure to commit to a regular writing practice was because I feared not being good enough as a writer, and from listening to my inner critic.

If you find yourself struggling to create a consistent writing habit, know that you are not alone. There is a way to begin to create a regular writing practice in your life.

It starts with building tiny habits.

So, what are tiny habits? Behavioral Scientist, Dr. B.J. Fogg says that a *Tiny Habit* is when you do something very, very small and you do it everyday.

For example, you might floss one tooth, do two push-ups or drink one sip of water.

Dr. Fogg says he sees it over and over again how people can change their habits consistently, all by beginning with one tiny habit change everyday(link to a blogpost on Tiny Habits and Dr. Fogg's Ted talk in the resources at the end of this chapter).

Thoughts of worry, fear and procrastination can all become a habit. Left unchecked, all three of these can become an unconscious loop that goes round and round in our heads. These self-sabotaging loops stop us from moving forward.

Many of our habits are triggered by things outside of us(spoken word, smells, sounds, etc.). Each trigger in your brain results in a behavior and every behavior results in a reward. According to Dr. B.J. Fogg, from a neuroscience perspective this is called a Habit Loop.

In other words, chances are very high that the fears

holding you back from achieving your goals are possibly ten, twenty or even thirty years in the making. These fears have become an unconscious pattern that repeats itself over and over again.

Most of the time when we have these fears, we don't know how to get out of that self-defeating cycle. This has definitely been my struggle. Sometimes we believe the negative words people said about our writing years ago, as if it's truth, and it keeps us stuck.

That happened to me when I was in elementary school and since that time I've struggled to get words on the page. My negative habit loop went something like this: *my writing isn't good enough; nobody will read my books; maybe I should quit now, I'll most likely fail at my writing dream anyhow.*

You can take steps to change your unhelpful habit loop. Building Tiny Habits everyday helps you to do that. I continue to take steps to change my unhelpful habit loops.

Everyday, I've chose to work on simple Tiny Habits and it's been so encouraging. I hope you find it useful for your writing journey.

Begin with three simple steps to start Tiny Habits everyday.

1.Take a sheet of paper and write down One Fear you realize has been holding you back from reaching your writing goals.

For example, for this step the number one fear I wrote

down was: *I have a big fear that my writing won't be good enough and that readers won't want to read my novels.*

Write down what your biggest fear is, so you see it in black and white, then move to step number two.

2.Write down One Tiny Action that you can take immediately, within the next 24 hours, that will move you away from that fear and towards the goal you want to achieve.

For example, since my big fear has been believing that my writing isn't good enough, I need to practice and grow my writing skills.

So I wrote down: My one tiny action that I've chose is to write for at least twenty-five minutes a day, without judging my words and writing whether I feel like it or not.

Then, I encourage you to celebrate your one tiny action. I do this by putting a quarter into the jar on my writing desk every time I complete a twenty-five minute timed writing session or Pomodoro.

A quick side-note: the pomodoro technique is a time management method developed in the late 1980s by Franceso Cirillo. A Pomodoro uses a timer to break down focused work into twenty-five minute intervals separated by short five minute breaks.

When I've saved up twenty or thirty dollars from the many timed writing sessions, then my hubby and I get to go on date. It's a great way to stay motivated!

. . .

3. After you have done that One Tiny Action for 7 days, add one more Tiny Habit to your everyday goals.

Simply add another really small habit to the habit you've already started. For example, when I've completed seven days of writing for twenty-five minutes everyday, I will add another twenty-five minutes of writing each day. So in total for the second week, I will have two pomodoros completed each day.

You can do something similar. If it works better for you to have word count goals instead of timed writing sessions, then start super simple. Consider starting with 250 words a day and do that for seven days and then the next week double that.

I think you'll really like the results when you begin with small habits on a regular basis.

As I've learned from different behavioural and neuro-scientists, what puts most people in the fight, freeze or flight mode is when they think of the Big Goal and then get overwhelmed with all they have to do.

What happens when we feel overwhelmed is that our brain switches to our biggest fears like: fear of success, fear of failure, fear of shame or fear of rejection, and many more.

As you build these tiny habits, what will happen is that you'll start to become a person who feels the emotion of fear, but you take a little step of action anyway towards what you want to achieve.

Remember, everyone feels fear. It's normal. It's how

you handle it and what you do with it that matters. So, take one small step each day in spite of the fear, anyway.

So, let's dive deeper into some specific areas and tips to overcome obstacles around lack of writing habits.

A) I don't have any extra time or I'm too tired to write most days.

Maybe you have a full time job and you're also a wife and mom(or husband and father). I get it. There isn't much time left and more than likely, you're very tired by the time the day is done.

The good news is that you can make writing super easy to fit into your day-to-day schedule. One way to do this, is to write on a Google doc(that's connected with your Gmail account, if you have one) on your smartphone.

You can also do this if you have scrivener on your computer and then all you do is get the scrivener app for your smartphone and you can sync the documents. That way you can write for ten or fifteen minutes - whenever you have a coffee or lunch break - and you can get quite a lot of words written during that time.

Experiment and find the time of day where it works best for you to write. Maybe you get up a 5am and write for thirty minutes before you get started for the day. Or maybe you're a night owl and write after everyone else is in bed. Do what works for you.

If you're feeling really exhausted, I encourage you to do what you can to create more energy for yourself. *As a disclaimer, I'm not a doctor or healthcare provider and exhaustion can be a symptom of many different medical conditions. So if you're dealing with exhaustion on a regular basis, please do talk to your healthcare provider.*

However, having lived with my own mother who suffered from deep exhaustion and depression and from my own experiences with both, I can safely vouch for the amazing turnaround to your body from taking out white sugar and white flour from your regular diet(I'm still working to make this a regular habit in my own life). I've seen people I know who have switched to a healthier way of eating, who have more energy.

Also adding a few short simple exercises to your body throughout the day can help with energy. For example, when you get up and move your body for a few minutes or go for a twenty minute morning walk. You might be surprised at how that re-energizes you.

I found that as I've started to switch my eating so that I'm eating more veggies, drinking green smoothies and more water, that my energy increases.

Experiment with different foods and see which ones are causing you to feel more tired. This might be one of the big keys to help give you more energy and increase your writing productivity like it was for me.

Also, I encourage you to set up boundaries for your writing time if you need to. For instance, I needed to have a conversation with my children where I told them I work best when I write in the mornings, so please don't disturb me during that time unless it's super important. Then, they know for the rest of the day they can talk or text me to chat. It works great.

Overall, ask yourself what things you can do to

improve your energy throughout your life. Examples might be: get enough sleep; create better exercise habits; set boundaries for your time; eat healthier foods, drinking more water and other ideas.

As you get more consistent with your writing habits, consider finding three separate times throughout the day where you can write for ten or fifteen minutes. Watch and see how these tiny habits add up and catapult your writing productivity.

B) I struggle to get words on the page most days. I get distracted and end up procrastinating on finishing my book.

There are a myriad of reasons why writers struggle to get words on the page and procrastinate to finish their books.

Sometimes we procrastinate because we have perfectionist tendencies and fear failure and so we resist starting or finishing a book until we feel 'ready.'

We think we've never been taught to write properly and we have all sorts of doubts about our writing.

Sometimes we procrastinate because of fear of the unknown and fear of readers not liking our books and then we freeze or find some other busy work so that we won't feel guilty about not writing.

I've experienced all of the above forms of procrastination and it can be very discouraging. So if you're discouraged or feeling hopeless about your writing, I want to encourage you don't give up and to keep reading.

My greatest desire for writers who read this book is that you will find one or two ideas that are like *"aha moments"* for you to try for yourself. Then you'll begin to unblock your creativity and the joy, momentum and fun will come back to you in your writing journey.

When we come to the root of it, our real challenge as writers can be traced back to mindset.

It's really important to dig deep and ask yourself what you are really afraid of when it comes to writing and finishing your book? Sometimes you might discover the root cause is something you hadn't realized before.

It wasn't until I started this writing journey and started reading different comments from other struggling writers that I started asking myself the hard questions like why was I so afraid to finish a book?

The answer of why I was afraid to finish a book came to me as I started writing morning pages...

I'm afraid to finish a book, because that means I will have to publish it for readers to read. And if I have a book out there in the world, it means anyone can read it. This means it's possible that someone will leave a scathing review or tell me to my face that this book is the worst thing they've ever read. Then I'll experience deep rejection and pain all over again, just like I did when I was in elementary school and my teacher told me my writing was like chicken scratchings.

That was my *"aha moment"* about my own deep rooted fear. I finally realized why I continued to self-sabotage and procrastinate on writing and finishing my books.

I had lots of ideas and could start writing the books just fine, but to finish the book was like I was trying to scale a hundred foot brick wall.

Somewhere along the way my subconscious mind had decided for me that it would protect me from pain and rejection... which also meant stopping me from finishing my book.

After this epiphany, I decided to double down on working on unblocking my creativity and shifting my mindset.

As you begin to shift into a different mindset - ideally the mindset of someone who has already solved the challenge you're having right now in your writing - then you'll be able to come up with a simple solution.

If you are overwhelmed about your book, try the tiny habits technique that we talked about earlier. When you break your book down into bite-sized chunks, it helps to bring clarity and makes it feel less overwhelming. Then you'll feel more at ease which will help you to get more done in a concentrated time.

If you're feeling distracted, first get very real with yourself as far as what needs to change. Ask yourself what is distracting you? Are you distracted by the Internet when you're writing? Consider getting an app for your computer like Freedom so you can't access the Internet while you're writing.

Are you distracted with phone calls, texts or by your children coming into your room while you're writing? I encourage you to have a conversation with people who support you.

Talk to your family and friends. Let them know that you won't be able to respond to them during certain creative time blocks of your day. I did this with my children, and it was really helpful.

Take the next step and figure out what is blocking you from finishing your book.

As you start to identify and untangle some of the writing challenges you're having, you'll begin to makes the changes you need to set yourself up for success in all your writing.

C) I'm stuck in the planning, writing or editing phase.

If you feel like you're stuck in the planning, writing or editing phase of writing, this typically this is about either being unsure on the 'how-to' of structure or you might be struggling with perfectionism in your writing.

If the area you're struggling in is about structure, this is a learning curve that all fiction and nonfiction writers need to learn. Every writer who finishes and publishes books to a deadline has a solid writing structure.

In fiction - if you are writing popular commercial fiction - most likely you are writing your book using Joseph Campbell's popular *Hero's Journey* as a guide. A great book for writers that simplifies the hero's journey is *Story Structure – Demystified* by Larry Brooks.

Similarly, in nonfiction you are also writing your thoughts on a specific subject, but sharing your own personal experience, which follows much of the *Hero's Journey*.

Learning story structure has a high learning curve that can feel frustrating, which in turn can make it a real struggle for writers to have a regular writing practice.

It's helpful to ask yourself questions to help gain clarity.

If you're a fiction writer, ask deeper questions of your two main characters. What is their greatest fear? What is their greatest wound? What is the biggest hindrance to reaching their goal?

If you're writing nonfiction, ask questions like: Who are my ideal readers? Who is that one person who is like I used to be, who really needs the solutions I can share with them? How will readers benefit from my book?

Hopefully asking those questions will be a good starting place to figure out a solid story structure so you can finish your book with confidence.

Take the time to read through books that explain story structure in an easy to understand way. I have listed resources at the end of this chapter that I've read through and have really helped to simplify story structure in my own writing.

If you struggle with perfectionism and you're procrastinating on finishing your book, start with tiny habits.

All you need to do is commit each day to write for a very short amount of time everyday - like ten or fifteen minutes - and you will have effectively started a tiny habit. If you do this consistently, then you'll start to see momentum and flow in your writing.

As you successfully write in short, focused time

blocks, you'll begin to increase your time blocks and the words written.

The beautiful thing is you'll start to feel more confident as a writer each time you complete a timed writing block. Then as a few weeks and months pass, it'll start to feel natural to you and you'll start to experience a new ease of creative flow in your writing.

I hope this chapter has helped shift your mindset to help inspire you that you can do this. You can clear away the roadblocks on your creative path and finish your book!

In the next chapter, we'll talk about what it means to calculate your strategy as an author to help you begin to grow and build your author business.

But, before you go to the next chapter, please do go through the questions and resources below to help you get clarity on how you can clear your creative path. For deeper insight on this, check out the companion workbook in print book format.

Something to try...

At the end of each chapter I try to offer some simple steps for you to begin to put into practice what you've learned.

I encourage you to take a few minutes to go answer the questions below and to check out the helpful resources.

I believe that going through these exercises will help bring the clarity and inspiration to finish your book.

. . .

Questions to ask yourself:

• What do you believe are your biggest blocks on the path to your writing goals?

• How do you limit yourself on your creative path to reach your goals and what beliefs are behind that?

• In what ways do you self-sabotage your goals?

• Have you tried any daily work to help you unblock your creative path like morning pages, daily journaling, affirmations, etc? If so, what?

Resources you might find helpful:

• A blogpost of simple steps on how to begin Tiny Habits: https://www.createastoryyoulove.com/tiny-habits

• Dr. B.J Fogg's *Tiny Habits website* on how to start small habits in your life.

• Tips on how to tap into your enthusiasm for your ideas by Mark McGuinness on his website: lateralaction.com.

• *Tips on the pomodoro technique* developed by Franceso Cirillo at francescocirillo.com.

• *Freedom Productivity App* to block the internet

• Podcast Interview with Colleen M. Story on how to unblock your writing path: https://www.createastoryyoulove.com/colleenmstory

• *Story Structure - Demystified* by Larry Brooks.

• *The Hero with a Thousand Faces,* by Joseph Campbell

• Podcast Interview on Giving Yourself Permission to Create with Pamela Hodges: https://www.createastoryyoulove.com/pamelahodges

• *The Anatomy of Story: 22 Steps to Becoming a Master Storyteller* by John Truby
• *Write Your Novel From the Middle: A New Approach for Plotters, Panthers and Everyone in Between* by James Scott Bell
• *The Plot Whisperer: Secrets of Story Structure Any Writer Can Master* by Martha Alderson
• Low cost online learning with Udemy.com

Chapter Three

Calculate Your Strategy

"Develop clear goals and objectives. Fully 80% of your success comes about as the result of being absolutely clear about what it is you are trying to accomplish." Brian Tracy

In this chapter we'll uncover how to get super clear on your strategy for writing and finishing your books and growing your author business.

As I've continued to write fiction and nonfiction books, I've realized how important it is to calculate a strategy that works well for you to help you reach your writing goals.

I learned how to do the difficult tasks first and how to

plan your strategy from reading Brian Tracy's helpful book *Eat That Frog*.

It certainly wasn't always like that for me. The struggle was real and very angsty for the first five years that I attempted to find my footing as a writer.

There were many days I cried tears of frustration trying to figure out this writing thing. I was trying to figure out story structure at the same time as I was trying to understand and find my own creative rhythm and learning how to focus.

There are many lessons I've learned along the way, mostly learned from mistakes or what not to do. It's because of my own struggles with resistance, distraction, perfectionism and limiting beliefs that I have become passionate about helping other struggling writers to finish their books.

So, that's why I wanted to share with you six simple steps that I've found helpful from what I've learned from mentors and through my own writing practice.

I hope this step-by-step map helps you to get really laser-focused and clear on your own strategy.

6 simple steps to help you calculate your strategy

As we learned in chapter one, an intense, burning desire for your reasons are critical to overcome obstacles and achieve your goals. In order for your desires to be intense enough, your goals must be very personal.

Your goals need to be something you really want for yourself, rather than just doing something that someone else wants for you or that you want to do to please someone in your life.

You must choose goals that resonate deep within you. In setting goals for your life, it's important to start with yourself first and then move forward. When you choose your true goals you start with your vision and your values.

Ask yourself: *what do I really want to accomplish with my writing?*

It's important to keep your eyes on the prize. Look into the future and see the goal out there from far away and get really clear on what you need to do to get there.

Remember, you can't reach your destination until you first get clarity on your vision and unblock your creative path.

As you begin the storyteller's journey, you have to get rid of the big tree trunks and boulders lying across your path so that you can see your way clear and take the next step.

The next step to take, after you have a clear vision and you've unblocked your creative path, is to calculate your strategy.

In simple terms, to calculate your strategy means that you are really evaluating the gap between where you are right now and where you want to go.

For example, maybe you've had an idea for your first book, and maybe you've even started to write. However, maybe you are scratching your head, unsure how to create a strategy to finish your book and launch it to readers.

If you're unclear on strategy, I hope these six steps below will be useful to you.

Listed below are six simple steps to help you gain clarity on your writing strategy.

1.Get crystal clear on where you want to go and the plan of action needed to get you there.

Getting clear on your strategy requires laser-like focus.

What is your focus?

This question could be asked another way. What is your goal? For most people reading this book, it will be to Finish Your Book or to become a full-time author.

I've noticed that with many writers just starting out, have a vague idea of the end result they are aiming for, but they don't set specific goals. For these first-time writers it means they don't make the shifts needed to reach their goals.

I definitely started writing with only vague ideas of what I wanted to write and a vision for my writing. Then, I started learning how important it is to write down a plan.

As you start to write down your writing dreams, it'll seem very unreal and almost impossible to reach your goals. But, don't give up. As you read on, you'll learn how to make your writing goals into simple do-able steps.

In setting goals, it's important to begin with general goals and then move to more specific goals.

The key here is to write down both general and specific writing goals in a notebook.

It's very inspiring to write down a master list of your

general goals that you've narrowed down from your dream list of goals you would like to accomplish.

It's compelling and motivating to see your vision written down on paper.

For example, some general goals might be: I want to make a living with my writing or someday I'd like to be a New York Times bestselling author.

Another way to approach general goals is to ask yourself what worries or bothers you in your day-to-day life that part of the solution would be writing the books you dream of writing?

For myself, I find it more motivating to ask where my biggest pain points are. Next, I ask what is the fastest and most direct way to solve those problems.

William of Ockham, a British Philosopher who lived from 1288 - 1347A.D., proposed a method of problem solving that has come to be known as Ockham's Razor.

"The simplest and most direct solution, requiring the fewest number of steps, is usually the correct solution to any problem."

Too many people make the mistake of making the solution to their pain point too complicated. The more complicated the solution, the less likely you will do it and the longer it will take for you to reach your goals.

Do your best to find the simplest, fastest and most direct route to reach your goals.

The best way to do that is to write down your goals, in a specific, measurable and time dated way.

When you set goals in this way, you are writing down the details needed to achieve your goal.

So, instead of only having a vague idea of the goals you

would like to reach, you will have a detailed plan on how to reach them.

That's why it's important to write down your overall master list.

This leads us to the second step.

2. Take a look at the boundaries within which your goal must happen.

It's too easy to skim over this point, but it's really important to write out what your boundaries are. Most writers have some sort of boundaries or parameters that are around their writing time.

For example, maybe you are a mom that works a full-time job from Monday to Friday and you have to always leave the house by 7:30am and you don't get home until 5pm. Also added to that, maybe you also have a husband and two young children that also need your attention.

When you add in the driving time for your work and getting the kids to school, maybe all you have is an extra 25 minutes to write in the morning(if you get up early) and maybe you can squeeze in 25 minutes of writing time at night and maybe you can figure out an extra two hours of writing time on the weekends. Let's say with each writing time block you get average of 400 words written.

Next, you would look at the time you have allocated for writing.

For example, let's say you only had a total of a little more than 6 hours writing time each week. Then we can figure out how much you can get done each week when you add up all your writing time blocks.

If you do the math on that, you'll know that each week you'll reach 5,600 words and within 30 days you'll have written 22,400 words. If you are writing a short novella or a short nonfiction book then you would be finished with the first draft of your book.

However if your book was full length at around 60,000 or 70,000 words, then in three months(or 12 weeks), you would have around 67,000 words written.

You would have a full length book finished in three months.

When you look at the end result that you want to reach for the book you're writing in this way, you'll understand what specific steps you need to take to make it happen.

It's super important to match your goal with the plan of action you need to take.

Take a moment right now to think through how your life is structured, and ask yourself what you can reasonably do in the time you have allotted to reach your writing dreams and goals.

As we continue to go through these next steps, I want to encourage you to commit to going through the questions at the end of this chapter. If you write down your answers, you will gain an amazing amount of clarity which will help you strategize to reach your writing goals quickly.

3.Figure out what a perfect day or dream day would look like for you.

You might have done this exercise before, but even if you have, I encourage you to do it again.

When I first did this exercise I was training to be a life coach and this was one of the questions I was encouraged to write down to help get clear on my vision.

It was super helpful to write down dreams and goals but also to write down what a perfect or dream day would look like for each hour of the day.

For example, here are some things my ideal day would include. I would get up at 6am and make myself green tea. I would sit outside and meditate, pray, say affirmations, read, and write in my journal.

Then I would grab my laptop and begin writing in my creative time blocks. I would do four focused twenty-five minute writing sessions with five minute break in between.

Then I would have a break and do something with my hubby for awhile. Then before lunch I would get in another 4 focused writing time blocks.

And then in the afternoon I would take an hour to check emails, check on marketing and then do stuff with my family like go hiking or water skiing and riding horses and read in the evening(I can't help it, it's my dream ;).

As you write out your perfect day, add some very personal details that would make your day great.

Be conscious as you write, where your writing is going to factor into your day. Have a plan of where you will schedule your writing blocks.

Maybe it works better for you to have specific days where you can schedule one to two hours of creative writing blocks and get some deep writing work done. If you can figure out some time for deep work, that will be super helpful to getting your book finished.

Map out each day of your week and ask yourself what you need to do so you can add those writing blocks into your schedule.

Something that might be helpful is to experiment on your writing location. Maybe you have a nice office at home where you write that works well, that's great!

If not, try writing at a coffee shop or library or you can set up a small desk in your home somewhere that's your writing desk. I've converted a corner of our bedroom into my writing space. It's quiet and a great space to write.

Consider the following questions to help you gain clarity on how to make your perfect writing day happen:

• What support do you need from your partner, children, friends, or job.

• What would help give you the time you need to write? (When you break down your perfect day by hour, it's easier to find the time you need to write).

• How can you close those gaps in your life that are draining your energy right now?(monitor your time on social media, time spent on the phone, time spent checking email, etc.).

• How does your perfect day match up with your original writing day? Think about how you have made more space to write. Ask yourself if you have given yourself enough space to write to hit your word count or if you are tracking your writing by minutes, check if you found the time to get your 25 minutes of writing done in the morning or evening?

• How can you make your writing habits consistent each day? Consider setting up reminders on your Smartphone and set up boundaries, habits, and routines. Put these little hooks in your day so you can really focus on your writing dreams and goals.

For example, if you're a fiction writer you might want to setup your computer the night before and write a short paragraph summary of the scene you will write, to prepare yourself to write first thing in the morning.

I encourage you to listen to the podcast interview with cozy mystery author Elizabeth Spann Craig, to learn how to start small and build a regular writing habit(You can find the link to the podcast listed under resources at the end of this chapter).

If you've gone through the questions above, you'll have a better idea of how you can make your perfect writing day happen for you.

Next, we'll do another exercise which will help you get really focused on the strategy for your writing goals.

4. Write down in detail the end result you want for this specific book.

If you look back at step number one at the beginning of this chapter focused on your overall dream for your writing.

This step is about focusing on the end result you want for this specific book you're writing now.

As mentioned before, it helps to narrow down your dream in detail for this specific book.

At this point, it will really help to look back at the start of this chapter so you can see what you wrote down in your notebook for your overall writing dream.

Is your dream to make a living as a fiction writer? Or maybe your dream is to write nonfiction books and be a coach or teach online courses. Or maybe you want to write a memoir or other inspirational books and be a speaker.

Whichever route you choose, the way to get there will look slightly different.

For example, if you want to make a living as a fiction writer and you are writing your first novel, you might want to consider writing a series.

From what I've learned from successful full-time Indie Authors like Bella Andre and Barbara Freethy, writing five books in the same series is recommended if you want to make good money with your fiction.

I decided to experiment with that technique by writing a romance series under pen name. Now that that first sweet romance series is finished, I can safely tell you that those five books have earned me the most money by far than any other books I've written.

The romance series is set in the same small town, and each book is focused on a different fairytale retelling. I got clear on the details of my writing plan and did it. The results were encouraging.

Writing in a series is also recommended if you're writing nonfiction books that are aimed toward a similar audience.

This is what I've done with this nonfiction series for

writers. My first book, *Write and Publish Your First Book*, was a general introduction for first-time writers, to introduce them to the possibilities of getting started writing their book and connecting with their readers. You can grab this first book at my author website: www.memorablefic tionbooks.com.

This book(*Finish Your Book*), is the second book in this series to help writers get beyond the obstacles on their path so they can finish their book(or books) and gain momentum with their writing.

The next book in this series for writers will be aimed at helping fiction writers to simplify the storytelling process.

In reality, there are many different pathways up the mountain as a writer. I encourage you to get as detailed as possible with your writing goals and dreams.

Essentially, you need to evaluate what you ultimately want for your author business. It's super helpful to read blogposts and listen to podcasts or YouTube videos by successful authors to help you learn what has worked for others. Then you can build your writing strategy on the details and ideas that you learn.

I encourage you to get really clear on the details for your own book and then write those details down in a notebook.

The next step will give you ideas on how to do that.

5. Write down a list of every step it takes to achieve your goal.

This step might seem redundant, but I can assure you

it's not. Doing this one step has given me incredible clarity and strategy on my writing goals.

It's so important to write down each step it will take to reach your goal.

You might be asking, why can't I just plan everything in my head? Why do I need to write it all down?

A method I used to try - which frankly didn't help - was to plan everything in my head without writing anything down.

What happened was I would end up quite overwhelmed, especially when I had a long list of things that needed to get done.

Then I started writing my plans and to do lists on paper, and most of the overwhelm went away. I encourage you to try it.

There are a few reasons to write down your step-by-step plans on what it will take to reach your goal.

First, there's a direct connection between writing down your goals and how solidly those plans sink into your subconscious mind.

Always think on paper. There's something quite amazing that happens between your head and your hand when you write out your plans in detail on paper before you begin anything.

When you write down your plans on paper, it sharpens your thinking and focus and stimulates your creativity.

Second, when you write details of your goals that are

really personal and compelling to you, you are more likely to do whatever it takes to reach them.

Third, according to time management experts, working from a list will increase your productivity by 25% from the very first day you start doing it.

Begin by making a list of what you need to do for the next twelve months to reach your writing goals.

This step is focused on how to reach your specific goal instead of your overall vision for your author business.

As you begin, you might find it helpful to refer back to your master list for your overall vision for your author business that we mentioned in step one of this chapter.

In the next step, you would break down your master list into what you need to do for each month for the next twelve months to reach the goal that is top of mind for you right now.

Then you would break your monthly list down into a weekly list. It's important to be specific about exactly when you are going to start and complete the tasks you've chosen to do for each week of the month.

Finally, make a list of daily activities you need to do each day. This is one of the most important lists you'll make. When you write down your list of your top three goals to do ∼ and you write them down preferably the night before ∼ your subconscious mind can work on your list while you sleep.

As you work at reaching your author related goals each

day, you can put a checkmark by each item on your list as you finish it.

What I find helpful is to keep a smallish yellow notepad beside me on my writing desk. Each new page is for the next day, and I write down my biggest 3 -5 items that I know need to be done that day if I'm going to reach my writing goals.

I write down how many pomodoros I was able to get done that day. I also write down if I need to write a blog-post or update my email newsletter that day.

I also write down at the beginning of every month revenue and expenses for the previous month. This makes filing income taxes less overwhelming.

It's helpful to write down the yearly, monthly, weekly and daily goals you want to reach.

Next step is to organize your list into a plan that works for you.

6. Organize and write down your list into a clear plan.

When you have set a crystal clear intention of what you want to accomplish, like we've done in the first part of this chapter, then it's important to zero in on your exact strategy to reach your writing goals.

Basically you're saying, this is my goal and that place in the distance is what I'm aiming for. If I want to hit that target, this is what I'll need to do to get there.

To make that image sharper and clearer, it's important to break down the simple action steps you need to take into an overall plan and then into small steps that you need to take each day.

Let's use the example below to breakdown the details:

What if your specific goal is to finish, self-publish and market your book to as many of your unique readers as possible in the next six months? How would you plan your strategy to do that?

Let's assume you are a first-time author who is just getting started writing a book and you don't have an author website or an email list.

We're also going to base this strategy on the fact that most people have really busy lives and not a lot of time to write.

What this means is that there are quite a few steps that would help you to reach more readers for your book.

If this is where you're at as a writer, no worries. These steps are all figure-out-able! At the end of each chapter are many useful resources listed to better help you navigate through each step.

I hope this plan helps you with ideas on how you can stay on track to release your book within six months.

Of course, you could always accelerate these goals if you figured out a way to give yourself more time to write each day.There are many indie authors I know who write and self-publish their books in a three to four month time period or faster. It's up to you and what works for your schedule how quickly you want to write and self-publish your book.

For the example below I went with a six month strategy to get everything done.

Below is a Hypothetical Example of a Six Month Strategy to write, self-publish and market your First Book:

I hope by writing the details of a possible six month strategy below, it will give you an idea of the sort of things that are important if you want to reach many of your unique readers with your book(s).

Week 1:

A. Brainstorm and outline your book idea.

1. Start with a basic book idea. Write down all ideas that pop into your head, even if it seems silly at first. I like to keep ideas in Evernote because I can sync it with my desktop computer and my iPhone.

2. Brainstorm your ideas and put them into groupings by creating a mind map or do this using index cards. Each of those groupings could be a chapter.

3. Flesh out more details for each chapter. You could write a short summary of what each chapter would be about here.

4. Sort the mind map or index cards you created into a more formal structure for your book. Here's where you can get rid of repeated ideas or chapters that don't make sense. Look also for information gaps that need more details.

5. Write your outline. I like to use Scrivener, but other options include using Word or Google doc. Just write down what you've worked out on your index cards or mind map summary.

B. Setup Your Author Website and Email List.

If you are just starting out as a first-time author, it's important to put your best foot forward right at the beginning.

A great starting place is to setup your author website and email list. Think of your author website as your home place on the Internet.

Your author website is where people come in to stop for coffee and chat with you. Yes they can also talk to you also on your social media channels like Facebook, but the wonderful thing about your website is that it's your home base. So if Facebook goes away tomorrow, you will still have your own place on the Internet for readers to find you.

Along with setting up your author website, you'll also want to setup your email list so that you can connect with those readers who connect with you and read your books.

It might help readers find and get to know you more if you write a blogpost once a month or so to start. By doing that you'll also create excitement for your upcoming book. I blog once a month on my fiction website, and I find that this is just about right so readers are kept up to date with what I'm writing and that way I also have more time to write fiction.

If you would like tips on how to setup your own author website and email list, I've written several blogposts and have recorded a step-by-step video tutorial on how to do that(you can find links to these resources listed at the end of this chapter).

Weeks 2 to 13:
   C. Write your book.
   1.Write your first draft. Remember we said in our previous example that if all we had were two writing time blocks of twenty-five minutes a day and two hours on the weekend to write we would have a full length novel in three months?

In this example, we'll stick with that idea of creating space in your daily schedule for a twenty-five minute writing block five days a week and then finding two hours of writing time on the weekend.

Focus on writing your first draft without thinking about editing your words. Just write the book. Let go of the need to make the book perfect and just write.

Basically, we have two types of brains when we're writing. The creative brain and the editing brain. It's really difficult to write in a creative flow when you allow the editing brain to kick in when you are writing.

If you worked on your outline as recommended for week one, you will now have an idea of what to write for each chapter. All you need to do is look ahead to the next chapters you've outlined and write whatever ideas pop in your head.

Just remember, more than likely you won't stick completely with your outline. However, having an outline or story beats written out does help you have a better idea of where your book is going.

Week 14:

D. Choose your book title, book cover designer and more.

You've just finished your first draft of your book. That's awesome! Sometimes it's good to take a break from the writing process.

You might find it helpful to take a few days between finishing your first draft and the editing phase to choose your book title, to begin looking for a graphic designer to create a wonderful book cover and to choose what your next book topic will be.

There are a few more ideas to begin as well, so you can stick to finishing your book in this six month time-frame.

1.Choose your Book Title. Write down possible ideas for your book title. Some helpful tips when coming up with a title are that: it's easy to remember, it creates curiosity or has branding potential.

If you like, you can look up keywords in the Google

Ads Keyword Planner Tool. This will help you see what is popular on Google for your specific book's title.

If you're writing a nonfiction book, I encourage you to discover what problems you know people are experiencing around the topic you're writing about and then provide great solutions.

If you've surveyed your readers on your email list or on social media, you'll have a better idea of what problems they need solutions to.

When you talk to your readers and or read through reviews of books in your genre or niche, that type of organic search will help you to find great keywords to use your title.

2.Write your Book Description and Blurb. Since your book is fresh in your mind, this is a great time to write out your book blurb that you'll put on the back of your book cover.

Also, it's helpful at this time to take the time to write a first draft of the book description you want to put on your author website as well as on digital retailers like Amazon, iBooks, Kobo and others.

3.Find a Book Cover Designer. Once you have your title chosen, begin to look for a graphic designer to create a genre specific and attractive cover for your book. Unfortunately readers do judge a book by its cover, so it's important to invest in a great book cover design.

If possible, I encourage you to invest the $200 to $300

to get a good book cover design. If you choose to hire a graphic designer for your book cover, you'll need a few hours to write out a brief summary of your book as well as what ideas you have for your book cover.

This will be a process that might take two months or so, so that's why it's important to get this started at this point in your book's process.

If however, you are on a shoestring budget, consider bartering with someone who does great design work or start learning how to design great book covers via YouTube tutorials(see the list of resources at the end of this chapter).

4.Hire a Book Formatter. If you plan on hiring a book formatter for your ebook or print Book, this is a great time to do that.

It's good to be able to let your formatter know the date your book will be finished so you can schedule their services ahead of time.

I've noticed that for print books especially, they can be tricky to get formatted correctly so it can be helpful to have someone design your print book for you.

However, maybe you prefer to do it yourself. I format my ebooks and print books myself. I started out using Scrivener to format my ebooks, but now I've switched to Vellum.

I love using Vellum for both ebooks and print books(If you are curious about these tools, just look for more information under the resources section at the end of this chapter).

. . .

5.Choose your next book idea. This is especially important if your first book is part of a series. Take a day or two to sketch out your ideas for the book and begin to map out a partial or full outline.

You could even pencil in a tentative deadline for when you plan to have the next book finished. I encourage you to do this, because it will help you to gain momentum for writing and finishing your books. This is what I've experienced as I've set my deadlines months in advance for my next book.

Try it for yourself, you might be pleasantly surprised at how this inspires and motivates you to move forward in your writing goals.

Weeks 14 to 20:
   E. Edit your book.
   Now that you've had about a week's break from finishing your first draft, that should help you come back to your manuscript and look at it with fresh eyes.

At this point, you should be about three and a half months into finishing your book.

The next few steps in this process will be the self-edits and going through suggested revisions from your editor and then proofreading your book.

1. Self-Edit your book. Take a week to go through your own self-edits of your book. In this step it's important to read through your manuscript with your editor's hat on.

The next step is to edit your original draft for flow, content and overall reading experience.

Just a note: if you are writing your first book, the editing process might take a little longer, simply because going over the details of your book is new to you. Which brings me to the second important point.

2. Email Advance Readers a copy of your self-edited manuscript: If you are asking advance readers to read through your book before you publish, then this is a great time to ask them to read it.

It's helpful if you can give them two to four weeks to read through it and offer their feedback. I encourage you to send at least one reminder email one week before you would like their feedback from reading your book.

3. Send your manuscript to an editor. Yes, this part can seem a little scary especially if this is the first time you've sent your book to an editor.

It's not fun to see grammar mistakes, typos or word omissions(I tend to do this a lot) that we need to fix, but these things are important to take care of before you publish your book.

It's super helpful to get feedback on other areas of your book, that might need to be tweaked. *It's important to send your book to an editor at least two months before you self-publish it so you have time to revise your book.*

Try not to let all the parts that need fixing get you down. It's normal for writers to fix things in their manuscripts, so you're in good company. Just do the work and then you can move onto getting your book into the hands of readers who are excited to read it.

If you aren't sure where to find editors or would like a few more editor suggestions, I've written out a list of editors in the resources section at the end of this chapter.

4. Review edits and polish the final draft. At this point you go line by line through the suggested edits your editor sends back to you.

Try to read your book out loud, as you can get a better idea of content flow when you do this. As an extra step you could also hire a proofreader or ask beta readers to read through checking for errors.

Many times another set of eyes on your content can be helpful to weed out any mistakes you might have missed. You can also use other proofreading tools which are listed in the resource section at the end of this chapter.

5. Consider comments from Advance Readers: By this point you will have received comments from hopefully all of your advance readers(if you've chosen to use advance readers).

If you haven't received any responses from your advance readers, email them one more time and give them a deadline to email you back with their comments.

It's also important to thank your advance readers for being willing to read your book before it's published and to let them know you appreciate them.

It's a wonderful gift to be connected with readers who take the time to read your book ahead of time and offer their feedback.

Week 21 - 22:

F. Add front and back matter to your book, format your book and finalize your book cover.

Only a few weeks left until you publish your book. This is the time to get more of the marketing details figured out.

1.Add front and back matter to your book and format your book. It is important to add specific pages to the beginning and end of your book.

Adding these pages will help the guide the reader through your content and will also help grow your author brand when you give your readers specific calls to action.

The beginning of your book should include these pages:

- A title page.
- A table of contents.
- A free reader magnet(This could be a cheatsheet, a short story or anything that relates to the book you're writing that will help grow your email list).

The back of your book should include these pages:

- Ask for reviews
- another offer for your free book
- a "more books by this author" page
- "about the author" page that includes website, email and other social media pages)
- a disclaimer and copyright statement

. . .

This step shouldn't take more than a day because you can look at a previous book you've published or look at the front and back matter of other books that are similar to your genre or topic.

In this step you should also format your book. If you are publishing as only an ebook, I recommend using Scrivener or Vellum. If you plan to publish as a print book also, Vellum makes beautiful print books.

If you are feeling ambitious, you could always learn to format your print book in Adobe InDesign, which you can have access to for a monthly fee. My husband learned to use this with my second book and we did the print formatting that way.

However if you choose to hire a book formatter, then your book should be nearly ready to go. Double check that you've sent them the front and back matter for your book and then after they've formatted it, it should be ready to go.

Double check that you have ePub, Mobi and PDF files formatted for your book, so that you can upload your book on all digital retailers.

The good news is once this step is done you will have a book that's ready to publish!

2. Finalize your Book Cover.

You'll want to double check with your book designer on how the book cover is coming along.

More than likely, by this point you've received a few emails already with attached photos of your book cover.

Perhaps, you have offered suggestions as well as

listened to what your designer recommends to make your book look even better.

If you have studied how to design books and have chosen to create your own book cover, then you'll also want to double check that you have the details listed below.

A few details to double check:

- Do you have a book cover for your ebook? Is the ebook title and author name readable in thumbnail size on digital retailer sites like Amazon?
- Do you have a book cover for your print book?
- If you're doing an audiobook, do you have a book cover(different size) for your audiobook?
- If you're using ISBNs, have given your book designer those numbers?
- That your back cover blurb on the back cover of your print book is eye-catching and that your book description is compelling and creates curiosity.

3. Write a newsletter to your email subscribers, write a blogpost, do a podcast or video on a topic related to your book's content.

During week one of this process, hopefully you setup your author website and created an email sign-up on your website for your readers to receive your newsletter and updates on new book releases.

Hopefully you've also had a chance to create your 'about page'(about the author) on your website. Another idea is to write two or three blogposts related to the theme of your book(whether your books are fiction or nonfiction), that will generate interest.

Or maybe you want to create a video slideshow or a book trailer of your book that you share on your blogpost or in your newsletter.

At this point in the process to finish, self-publish and market your book, you are only three weeks away from your book release.

This is a good time to send an email to your subscribers on your email list. Even if you only have a small list right now, it's still great to connect with them once every two weeks or so at the beginning so they can get to know you.

Do your best to make your emails something your readers look forward to by making them interesting and fun. Maybe you create and email a fun character quiz of your main characters in your fiction book. Or maybe you create a helpful checklist or cheat sheet related to your nonfiction book.

Remember that it takes many months and sometimes a couple of years to grow your email list of readers that really connect with you and your books.

So don't give up when your email list is small at the beginning. Everyone starts at zero. Just keep adding value to your readers and show your personality in each email, blogpost or video you share.

There are many ways you can create interesting emails for your subscribers and that way they will really look forward to your emails!

. . .

4. Create your newsletter email launch plan for your new book.

When you are first starting out as an author, you biggest goal is to let readers know that your book exists.

There are quite a number of ideas you can experiment with to get as many eyeballs as possible on your books, a few of which I list below.

Some ideas to attract the attention of your readers:

• free book giveaways.

• group promotions with other authors in your genre.

• price promotions(launch your book at $0.99 cents).

• Grow your email list with a free book offer like a short story or novella in your genre when they subscribe to your list. Or if you're writing nonfiction, offer a free checklist, cheatsheet, video training or short nonfiction book related to your website's topic they can get when they sign up on your website.

• make a books page on your author website.

• create a coming soon page on your author website for the next books you plan to write.

• Write a blogpost of the first few chapters in your new book.

Ideas for your email book launch...

• standard launch announcement a few days before your book releases.

• send another email with what your family is doing or about you and your pets(or something else fun and authentic) then share an excerpt of the book.

• On book release day send a blurb about the book and pic of the book cover.

• A few days later send an email asking 'have you started reading yet?'

• invite them to a giveaway/book club/ offer for a free book that's part of your launch email sequence.

• blogpost that is sent as a RSS campaign: could do a quiz for which character in the book they like best?

• Two weeks after they have the book, you could ask readers to review the book and add link in email to review page.

Remember it is super important to be your authentic self and focus on building a relationship with your readers. Focus on the value you offer your readers.

This is why your wonderful self is the most important thing you bring your readers. To do this well, it helps to focus on writing to one reader at a time, and chat with them like you're sitting across from them having a coffee.

Connect with your readers in a way that they'll want to reply back to you and then respond to them. It helps when your readers feel a little like you are giving them a warm cyber-hug.

Week 23:

G. Proofread final files in all formats and write out final description for digital retail stores like Amazon and upload book files for ebook and print.

At this point in our six month book launch schedule, you are only one week away from your book release.

1.Proofread your final manuscript in all formats. This is after your book has been self-edited and an editor has gone through it with a fine-tooth comb. This is the fun part where you get to see what your book looks like on different digital devices.

It's really helpful to see how your book's table of contents, chapters and end matter show up when you see it through Kindle or ePub previewer.

Take a close look at your book on both reading platforms, scrolling through the pages and write down any formatting issues. Fix them and keep previewing until you think your book is ready to be published.

There is a helpful resources section at the end of this chapter for links on how to preview your book on ePub and Mobi.

2.Write out the sales description for Amazon and other Digital Retailers. You might have written out a first draft of a sales description to put on the digital retail stores like Amazon, Kobo, iBooks and other places.

In this step we're going to tweak your description for your book, so readers who are looking at your book are compelled to keep reading and buy your book.The following are tips you might find useful for both nonfiction and fiction.

Tips for writing a compelling fiction description:

• Pick your main conflict vs. trying to summarize your entire plot.

• Focus on the conflict that most of your readers in your genre would most identify with.

• Be willing to simplify and boil your ideas down to what's essential.

• Look at Amazon reviews to tweak your description in the language that connects with readers of your genre.

Tips for writing a compelling nonfiction description:

• Identify the problem: what do readers of this topic struggle with most everyday?

• Hint towards a possible solution: in what ways do you recommend people overcome this obstacle?

• Offer your book as the solution: share what benefit your book provides over other books on this topic.

• Look at Amazon reviews from other books on a similar topic and tweak your description so that it's in the language of your readers.

I search for kindlepreneur.com online and use the book description generator to form the html coding that I need to stick my description into Amazon when I upload my book there.

· · ·

3.Upload your book to Kindle Direct Publishing(Amazon), Kobo, Google Play, KDP Print (for print books) or use Draft2Digital or SmashWords to upload your book to distribute it to different digital retail stores.

Upload your ebook: This is the exciting part, because you finally get to upload your book to retail stores! If you'd like you can self-publish directly to Amazon through KDP Direct Publishing or to Kobo or Google Play.

You can self-publish direct to iBooks too, it's just a little more involved process. For the rest of the digital stores like Nook, Tofino and others, you might find it easier to use a distributor like Draft2Digital or Smash-Words to get your book into those other retailers.

I've added the links to each of the above digital retail stores in the resources at the end of this chapter. If you're unsure how to upload your books, they have video tutorials on YouTube or you can do a Google search to learn how to do this.

Once you've uploaded your book, your book cover and you've added your book description and categories and set your book's price, you should be ready to go.

Normally it takes between twelve to twenty-four hours for your book to be live for readers to buy it.

. . .

Upload your files for Print Book: You can format your print book yourself and upload it to Amazon's new KDP Print to self-publish print books.

Since CreateSpace is no longer an option for print books, give KDP Print a try(you can find a helpful article on KDP Print at the end of this chapter).

Sometimes formatting for print books can be a little tricky and can take a few tries to get it right. You could always hire someone to format your print book for you. I did this with my first novel, and it saved me a lot of time.

If you choose to hire out your formatting or if you do the formatting yourself, then when your book is finished being formatted for print, just upload the book to KDP Print.

Simply select the "Add a New Title" link and choose the "Guided" option when it asks for what setup you prefer. From there, KDP Print will walk you through the publishing process.

To evaluate which printing option is right for you, you might find it helpful to read a blogpost that will walk you through how to set up your print book at the end of this chapter.

4. Add the book to your author profile on Amazon. You want to make sure all your books are listed on your author profile.

Your author page acts like a mini-website on Amazon and it's where readers can learn more about you and the books you offer.

It's simple to use. Just go to Amazon's Author Central

and find the "books" tab and select the "add more books" button. Then find your newly published book and choose the "This is my book" option.

Within a couple hours your book will automatically appear on your author page.

5.On your book release day, remember to email your subscribers to let them know of your new book. It's especially important to let those people who connect with you on your email list know when you have a new book release.

It's also great if you can offer your subscribers a lower price point on your book if they buy it when it's first released.

One strategy is to have a limited time during your book launch where the price of your book is $0.99 cents and then increase your book to $2.99(or any price point up to $9.99 if you want the 70% royalty) right after your book launch is complete.

They key here is to follow through with your promise that the price will go up on a specific date.

That way your readers come to trust that when you say a book is at a lower price for a limited time that you really mean it.

6.Do your best to get at least 5 reviews of your book. It's important to have a few reviews of your book.

Many readers aren't very interested in buying books that don't have reviews.

Most authors don't like to ask for reviews, but I encourage you to step a little out of your comfort zone and reach out to readers like:

• People who have read previous books you've written. A great long-term strategy is to slowly build a 'street team' of people who like your books and are willing to leave reviews.

• Bloggers, podcasters and other influencers in your specific niche.

Please, avoid swapping reviews with other authors or even worse, paying for reviews of your book. This not only is misleading for readers, but can get you in trouble with Amazon and other digital retail stores.

That being said, do ask for reviews from your email list, from posts on social media or anywhere else that you connect with your readers.

7. Interact with readers. During your book launch you'll likely get quite a few questions, comments, emails and reviews. It's super important to follow up with each reader.

Remember these are readers who are supporting your work, so it's your job to thank them and give them as much help as you can.

That's the end of this hypothetical six month strategy to finish and launch your book.

I hope you found these steps helpful as you finish your book and plan your own strategy.

After reading this chapter, you might be feeling a little overwhelmed at the many steps involved in writing, finishing and marketing your book. If that's you, don't worry, you are not alone.

At first glance when you take in everything at once, it does seem a bit daunting, but this is where doing a 'small bit of something' everyday to take action on your plan comes into play.

We'll talk more in depth about setting intentions for the goals we're shooting for in the next chapter. I look forward to seeing you there.

Meanwhile, before you turn the page, I'd love to encourage you to take a minute or two to write down some of your own action steps under the 'something to try' section below.

I promise you, writing down your steps(no matter how small) will make all the difference to finishing your book and getting it into the hands of your readers.

Something to try...

At the end of each chapter I try offer some simple steps for you to begin to put into practice what you've learned.

I encourage you to take a few minutes to go answer the questions below and to check out the helpful resources.

I believe when you go through these exercises, it will help bring the clarity and inspiration to finish your book.

· · ·

Questions to ask yourself:

• Review what you wrote down for why you want to write from chapter one. Next, ask yourself what are real meaningful goals for you? (examples might be: freedom, location independence, leave a legacy, time with family, etc).

• Write out what your 6 simple steps are, to get more clarity on your writing strategy. (It'll be helpful to review this chapter again).

• What are some ideas for your 6 month strategy to get your book written, published and marketed to your readers? I encourage you to take 30 minutes to write down your ideas.

Resources to help you:

• *Eat That Frog:21 Ways to Stop Procrastinating and Get More Done in Less Time* by Brian Tracy

• Get your FREE Self-Publishing checklist PDF at the link below: https://www.createastoryyoulove.com/the-storytellers-roadmap

• Video Tutorial on how to write your book using Scrivener: https://www.createastoryyoulove.com/scrivener/

• Video Tutorial on formatting your ebook and print book with Vellum: https://www.createastoryyoulove.com/vellum

• How to setup your wordpress author website video tutorial: https://www.createastoryyoulove.com/video-tutorial-wordpress-website

• *30 Day Author: Develop a Daily Writing Habit and Write Your Book in 30 Days (or Less)* by Kevin Tumlinson

• *How to Market A Book: Third Edition* (*Books for Writers Book* 2) by Joanna Penn

• Google Keyword Planner Tool to help with keywords for your book

• List of recommended Book Designers: https://www.createastoryyoulove.com/book-cover-design/

• List of recommended Book formatters: https://www.createastoryyoulove.com/formatting

• List of recommended Book Editors: https://www.createastoryyoulove.com/editors

• Learn how to Preview your ebook on Kindle OR how to preview your ePub book here.

• Learn how to create your amazon author page here: https://www.createastoryyoulove.com/amazonauthorcentral

• Learn how to setup your book description on digital retail stores: https://www.createastoryyoulove.com/bookdescriptiongenerator.

Chapter Four

Commit to the Writing Process

"One day you just have to start and what you do that day is the beginning of success or failure. I cannot write an entire book today, but I can write one page.

You can begin.

Dreams coupled with the firm intention to manifest them take on a steely reality... It is when we fire the arrow of desire, when we actually start a project, that we trigger the support for our dream."

Julia Cameron, Walking In This World

At this point in your book writing process, it's important to remind yourself again why you care so much about writing this book.

Take a minute and think back when you had the initial spark to write this book.

What was the compelling reason or vision you had in your mind, that made you tell yourself: *That's it. That's the story I have to write. I know this story wants to be told in my own words.*

I know how it feels to have a story that wants to spill out of you. That was my experience with my first historical romance, *Answering Annaveta.*

This series of novels was sparked by my dad's family's journey and the sacrifices they made while living in Russia and then leaving Russia in the early 1900s to travel to Canada.

Their angsty journey of family sacrifice and strength during hard times was inspiring and I felt it was a story that needed to be told. So I poured myself into writing it. Maybe you have a story that you feel compelled to write too.

I encourage you to think back to when you first had the idea to write your book. Is it the theme(*examples: an underdog overcomes against all odds or love conquers all*) that inspires you to write this book? Maybe it's a deeply personal story in some way and it must be written.

If your story compels or inspires in a deep way, that will really accelerate your writing process.

This compelling reason is what you need to keep coming back to, to help you continue to write and finish your book.

When you care enough about your vision that you're willing to sacrifice or move around some things in your life so that you can write, then it's far more likely that you will do the hard work and do it often enough that you will reach it.

It's time to count the cost and decide to commit to finishing your book.

In chapter three, I shared an example of what it would take to write and finish your book in a six month time-frame. This was based on an example of a first-time writer just beginning their author journey.

There were quite a few details to figure out including setting up your website, your email list and not to mention finding the time to focus on writing your book everyday.

After reading that chapter, hopefully you could see yourself making room in your life to finish writing that story that perhaps you've been talking about writing for years.

When we talk about counting the cost, it means to be wise and to develop a good perspective of the details involved before setting out to do a big project.

Many times in our lives, we don't have the resources or fortitude we need to be able to finish something.

We have to realize that writing our book(s) will mean that we'll need to give up some things to make the time and have the resources necessary we need to write and finish the book.

When you get out into the middle of the ocean of what you said you were going to do, at some point there will come a time when there is no shore and there will be no one out there but you and you've got to keep going.

Sometimes we have a book idea we want to write, but aren't sure how to really get it done. Counting the cost and learning to commit is really about gaining a sense of clarity on this new decision to finish a book.

But the big question is, how do you actually finish that project you care deeply about?

Learning to combine the motivation to start your project and also having a way of evaluating your goals throughout your process will help you finish.

To do this, it can be helpful to think of how you will empower yourself not only to start, but to take consistent action until you reach your goal and finish what you started.

Outcome Based Thinking and Method Based Thinking

Outcome Based Thinking

In order to get anything done, it's important to understand on a deeply personal level, what the benefits will be for you when you map out your goal.

When you understand how finishing this specific project will benefit you - in this case writing your book - knowing this will give you a strong drive and motivation to do what it takes.

This really could apply to any goals and results you have for your life, but in this book we will continue to focus on your goal of finishing your book.

When you have Outcome Based Thinking, you will be empowered to start and take the

action necessary to achieve the results you want.

Knowing what the results and benefits you'll receive at the end of your journey, will empower you to do the hard work to push past obstacles that will try to hinder or stop you.

It is important to be clear on the results you are looking for, simply because how else would you know which strategic steps to take to get it done?

You can let yourself be inspired by the benefits you will receive after you finish this project.

3 Ways to Inspire Yourself with the Benefits of Finishing your Book

There are many ways to move toward results based thinking and motivate yourself with the results and benefits of finishing your book.

Some examples of the benefits of finishing your book:

- fulfill your dream of writing a book
- begin your career as a writer
- grow a following of readers that have a relationship with you and who love your books
- earn a part-time or full-time income from writing
- leave a legacy

Of course those aren't all the benefits you can receive from writing a book. Some other benefits might be things we can't control, like having the respect of other writers in the industry or becoming a New York Times bestselling author.

In the above situations, all we can do is to consistently do the hard work of writing books, marketing them and connecting with readers and other authors in our niche. Then at some point maybe we'll see the results we want.

I encourage you to read through the three ways I've listed below, to inspire yourself to write and finish your book. Or, if none of those ideas work for you, figure out a way that works to motivate you get the results you want.

1.Write on a whiteboard to map out your strategic plan and the benefits you want to receive along the way.

Put the whiteboard in a place where you see it everyday so it inspires you. Write your vision statement at the top and repeat it everyday before you write.

2.Create a Vision board of your plan and the benefits you will receive when you finish your book (or book series).

Draw pictures, cut out pictures from magazines or find other pictures that inspire you and put them on your vision board. Again, write out your vision statement and put it somewhere in large letters where you will see it everyday.

3.Create a webpage on your author website, where you write down and show pictures of

the results you dream of getting for finishing your book or books.

Most likely this will not only inspire you, but readers or other writers that come to your website too! I encourage you to write out your vision statement in different colour font on your webpage.

It's important to be clear of the details along the way to help you reach your goal. What are the simplest steps to help you reach your goal? How will you respond to different obstacles as they show up to hinder your progress?

You don't need to know every single obstacle you'll face to reach your goal, but it is helpful to map out potential obstacles and figure out ways you could navigate around them when they do show up.

Side Note: *You can count on the fact that obstacles will show up, but you can figure out your way around them.*

Method Based Thinking

It's not enough to focus on the end result of reaching your goal to finish your book. You also need to think about how you are going to get there.

When you focus on the steps you need to take to reach your end goal, this helps you to accelerate your writing.

When you have Method Based Thinking, you will be empowered to focus on each step you need to take so you can finish what you have started.

This is really about getting super clear on the steps you need to take in order to achieve your goal, which in this case is finishing your book.

In the previous chapter, we laid out an example of what it would take to write and finish your book if your goal was to self-publish it in a six month time-frame.

This example of a simple step-by-step strategy is a way of evaluating each step needed to get your book finished in six months.

Maybe your goal is different than finishing a book in six months. Maybe as you consider what you all have going on in your life, you think you'll need a year. Or, maybe you want to get your book written and self-published within a three month time-frame. That's great.

The next step you would need to take, would be to figure out what you need to do to - including what you'll need to sacrifice - in order to reach your goal.

It's not easy to sacrifice some things we love, in order to finish our book. I found it difficult to give up that extra hour of time in the evenings with the family, but it's what I needed to do so I could finish my books.

Maybe for you, the only time it's quiet in the house is early morning and you need to get up thirty minutes earlier to write.

As you are willing to do whatever it takes to finish your book within the schedule you've set for yourself, you'll find not only will you achieve your goal but you will also raise your confidence level as a writer. *Bonus!*

To put yourself in the best position to reach your goals means that you will have to plan your daily, weekly and monthly activities so that you have given yourself the best chance possible to be successful.

Remember to make each of your steps small and easy to do.

I've noticed that when I take action steps that are small enough, I have a better chance of reaching the daily or weekly goal I've set.

3 Small Steps to Carry Out Outcome Based Thinking

Sometimes things show up in our day-to-day lives that we need to rethink in order to give ourselves the best chance to reach our goal of finishing our book in the time-frame we originally mapped out.

It's helpful to have a daily or weekly time set aside on your calendar, when you think about how your goals are coming along.

There are three steps that if you do them weekly, will help you notice what is helping or hindering you to reach the results you want.

Every Sunday I usually take thirty minutes to rethink the three steps below, getting rid of obstacles and tweaking what needs to be made better.

You can do this on Saturday or Monday, but whichever day you choose, I hope this helps you to evaluate and tweak your own writing process each week.

Step 1: Rethink the past seven days to see what went well and what could be improved.

Writing by hand in a notebook or notepad, take a look back over each day in the past week. How many days did you write? Maybe you only wrote for three days in the past week. That's okay, don't get down on yourself.

Just figure out how to find a better time slot to write or get rid of something else that's unnecessary in your day like TV time, scrolling through Facebook, checking emails, or whatever else.

Step 2: Plan and write down your top three goals you want to reach for today.

At the start of each day, take five minutes and visualize the action steps you want to reach that day.

See yourself doing each task, starting with the first one. It helps if you can imagine possible obstacles that might pop up and figure out ways that you can get around them. To stay focused, I write in twenty-five minute time blocks with a five minute break between each writing session. I do four of these in a row and then take a break. This helps me stay focused.

Maybe you only have time for one time-block in the morning and another one at noon or in the evening, that's okay. Your writing time block could only be five or ten minutes when you first get started. That's great. It's actually a good idea to start small, because then there's less resistance and that increases the likelihood that you'll write.

The important thing is that you have planned your day in advance and set focused writing sessions to reach your writing goals so that you can finish your book.

. . .

Step 3: Create an action plan for the coming week.

It is super helpful if you plan the action steps you need to take for each of the next seven days. Take the time to map out your overall weekly strategy using pen and paper. Create a timeline of when each chapter needs to be finished, so you can reach your end goal.

To inspire and motivate you to do the action steps each day, take five minutes and visualize yourself doing each action step for the next seven days.

See yourself reaching each goal you've set for yourself(maybe you've written two or three chapters that week), and let yourself feel the joy and sense of accomplishment from reaching your goals at the end of each week.

To help you reach your destination, it's important to combine both outcome thinking and step-by-step thinking.

Combine Outcome Based Thinking and Method Based Thinking

To be super effective to start your book and also finish it, you need a combination of outcome based thinking and method based thinking.

When you have outcome based thinking, you are focused on your desired outcome. This is a great place to start. But we also need to know the method of achieving the result we want.

In other words, it's important to know the end goal you're shooting for, but you also need to know the steps it will take to reach your goal. This is why you need step-by-step thinking alongside of outcome thinking.

When you combine knowing your desired outcome with the step-by-step process on how you have to do it, you will reach the finish line quicker.

When you are able to see the outcome you desire and combine that with the simple steps to get there, you'll be more committed to doing the work you have to do.

Choose to Commit

"You must finish what you start."
   Robert A. Heinlein, from Heinlein's Rules

The purpose of this book is to help you go from *I am stuck or procrastinating on writing my book* to *I am finished writing my book.*

So far, I hope you've found the different ideas to overcome resistance and strategies to finish your book useful.

In the end though, your desired result - that of finishing your book(s) - comes down to one very important choice: the moment you choose to be a committed writer who will finish your book.

It's the moment you've decided that there is no other option, that you will do whatever it takes, for as long as it takes, to write and finish your book.

It's vital that you choose to be *all in*.

As I'm sure you know, there are much easier things you could be doing than writing and finishing your book.

But, if you are wavering on making this decision, I

encourage you to *go back to your compelling reason* that hopefully you wrote down(from chapter one) of why you must write and finish this book.

Some of my lessons learned on this writing journey, is that any meaningful project always calls for more effort, costs more money and takes much longer than we originally thought.

It's much too easy to let these factors discourage us along the way. Somehow we believe that our high level of excitement will cause us to finish our book in a hurry. The truth is that you might finish your book in less time or it might take you longer than you thought.

When you are learning any other business or job, it also takes time and effort, costs money and sometimes takes longer than you thought too.

The difference in writing your book, is that you not only make an income from it, but you leave a legacy for those you love. I often remind myself of all the amazing benefits of writing stories I love when I feel discouraged in the writing process.

I encourage you to keep those positive benefits of writing and self-publishing in front of you each day you sit down to write.

The critical question to ask and answer for yourself is: *If it takes less or more time than you originally thought, will you still choose to commit?*

When you make the choice to shift your perspective from a sometimes-writer to a pro-writer, you begin to see yourself and your future in a better light.

You begin to realize the potential of writing and finishing this book and others. At sometime in your life, more than likely you've chosen to commit to something before, whether it's a job, losing weight or to a relationship.

Commitment doesn't mean that you are sort of interested in something. Commitment means that you have thought through what this will cost you in time, resources, and what kind of sacrifice it will require of you on a personal level and you've decided you're in.

To commit to something means that you have strategically thought out the steps in process, what you need and what will be required of you and you've made a promise to yourself(and possibly to others) that you will do this thing.

One of the hardest parts of making a commitment is to realize that this will now become a regular routine or habit in your life.

When you make this perspective shift from *I have an idea to write my book* to *I choose to be all in and commit to finish my book,* you'll see your book project in the right light.

This is the point when you begin to take action on your writing dream, which is both exciting and terrifying all at the same time.

What it means to commit to your writing dream

Much like a commitment to a regular day job, or starting a small business, a big reason why one writer is successful and another writer doesn't progress nearly as much, is because of one key: commitment.

A committed writer will work extra hours even while they have a regular job or run a business or a household and continue to write undeterred by the distractions of life.

When I first started writing, it was a on and off again sort of commitment, which is why it took my a little over five years to write and self-publish my first novel. With the second novel I was able to cut that time by about one third. The difference was I was more committed.

Writing on a regular schedule is what happens when you are committed, and the results can be amazing.

For example, an author who writes an average of 500 words a day(five days a week), for three years will produce an amazing three hundred and ninety thousand words. That's about two full length books a year.

To reach your desired outcome to finish your book(and finishing more books if that's your goal), will mean a big commitment.

This won't be determined by luck, but by your willingness to make a weekly and daily commitment to reach your goal.

Stick to your commitment in spite of resistance

When you choose to commit to finish your book, you can count on obstacles and resistance to attempt to hinder your progress.

Daily reminders of the commitment you've made to finish your book will help you, especially on days when you feel discouraged by the long process. Or when you must choose to live a simpler lifestyle and keep your expenses down so you can write. Or when you launch your book and it doesn't sell as fast as you'd like.

I get it, I really do.

More than likely, your challenge (much like mine has been) will be to continue with the same level of commitment that you started with ,even after the first spark of enthusiasm has left.

That's why it's important to remind yourself daily of your compelling reason why you are writing this story and to speak positive affirmations into your life.

You know, deep inside of you, that you were meant to write this story. You know that there are readers out there who are just waiting to read your story and be inspired. Are you ready to commit to finish your book?

The next step to help you when resistance strikes is to write down your affirmations and goals, then say them out loud and act on them everyday.

3 Key Daily Practices to Beat Resistance and Stick to Your Commitment to Finish Your Book

When I started writing down and saying out loud positive affirmations for my writing two years ago, I was quite skeptical.

I didn't think it would help me at all, but I thought if the worst that happens is that everything stays the same, then I haven't lost anything.

So I set my alarm on my iPad to go off everyday and spoke out loud the positive messages I wanted to tell myself. A couple of those affirmations were: *I am excited and passionate about my writing* and *I write to bring joy, hope, love and change to the world.*

As I continued to read books on how to begin a positive mindset routine, I happened upon the book, *Miracle Morning For Writers* by Hal Elrod, Steve Scott and Honoree Corder.

From reading this book, I learned how to start each day in a way that would help me shift my focus in a positive way. I

n a podcast interview with bestselling nonfiction author Steve Scott, he shared how setting positive routines and habits has helped him as well as authors he knows to gain the peace of mind, clarity and motivation they need each morning(*you can find that podcast interview listed in the resources at the end of this chapter*).

At the beginning of this book, I touched briefly on how to gain clarity for your vision. As important as that is, it isn't quite enough to be able to beat the resistance that will show up every time you sit down to finish your book.

There are three key practices that will gradually help you focus, shift your mindset, and find the motivation to write, if you work on them daily.

1.Daily Affirmations:

The definition of Affirmation is: *the act of validating or confirming; a positive assertion; to express a strong belief in something or a dedication to something.*

Many times in our lives, we accept negative or limiting beliefs about ourselves either from people we respect, or from our own inner critic. Very often, these negative messages, began in our early years and have been a mindset we adopted without thinking about it.

Without realizing it, we have been programmed to believe, think, act and talk to ourselves in a certain way. When we come face-to-face with a crisis or difficult circumstance, our mind habitually defaults back to unhelpful self-talk. This way of thinking is revealed throughout all aspects of our lives, including our writing.

This is why, to become better writers, we need to retrain our minds to think and speak only what we want.

When you write down and say out loud your affirmations, it helps that shift to happen in your mind. As you regularly repeat to yourself who you want to be, what you want to accomplish and how you are going to get it done, your subconscious mind will begin to shift your beliefs and your actions will soon follow.

Science has proven that affirmations, done correctly, are one of the most powerful ways to accelerate change and become the person you want to be to achieve what you want in your life. Many times however, people have tried affirmations and have been disappointed with hardly any results.

When affirmations don't work, it is often because they lack two key elements. Successful affirmations need to be rooted in truth, and stated using active language instead of passive.

Write down the desired result you are committed to doing(not just what you want) and the action you are committed to taking: For example: *I write and finish the first draft of my book by _____ (date), and I am totally committed to writing for 25 minutes each day from 5:30 a.m. to 5:55 a.m. and to write for another 25 minutes in the evening from 8:00 p.m. to 8:25 p.m. until first draft is finished.*

Next, keep your commitment in front of you all the time. Write your affirmation down on an index card that you put by your computer, writing desk or on your bathroom mirror.

Read and speak your affirmations out loud every day, letting your authentic emotions like excitement and determination to lead the way.

When you speak your affirmations out loud everyday - and it becomes part of your routine everyday - only then will you begin to see results.

I really hope you give this a try. The longer I've done this, the more my mindset has shifted, resulting in more action steps that move me closer to what I want. I'm convinced that if you do these exercises on a regular basis, you will find yourself moving closer and closer to the results you desire.

Take a minute to write down your own affirmations with the desired result you are committed to take action on every day, and watch as your mindset shifts and you begin to see the results you want.

2.Daily Visualization:

The definition of Visualization is: *formation of mental visual images; the act or process of interpreting in visual terms or of putting into visible form.*

Put simply, this is a way of using your imagination to create what you most desire. It's well known that Olympic athletes or top performers add space in their day for visualization as part of their daily practice.

This accelerates a shift in their mindset that helps them to improve their abilities by seeing themselves doing the action steps.

You might be asking what you would visualize that would help you in your writing practice?

Many times as writers we are limited by our memories of past results that weren't so good.

With creative visualization, you can map a new picture in your mind that will give you a compelling and exciting future for your writing journey.

It's helpful to practice visualization after you've read your affirmations as you are in a positive mindset and you are already in a focused state of mind.

It's simple to do. Just sit comfortably and close your eyes taking in slow, deep breaths. Then for the next five minutes, form a picture in your mind of the specific actions(example: writing each day) you need to do to make your short and long term goals a reality.

If you want to, take another five minutes and visualize the results(*example: holding your book in your hands*).

To visualize the actions, you could see yourself in your mind's eye writing each morning in a regular routine you've set up. Imagine yourself writing a short summary each day of what you will write.

Picture all the great ideas flowing into your mind and then onto the blank page. It's also helpful to picture yourself stopping yourself from distractions like email or social media. Picture yourself quickly getting back to writing your book.

One of the most important aspects of visualization is to give yourself the freedom to picture your life without limitations. Ask yourself what you would choose if you could have, do or be anything you wanted?

Taste, see, feel, hear, touch and smell all the details of your vision. When you use all your senses to make your visualization more compelling, your resolve to take the necessary actions will become stronger.

As you continue to write and finish your book, visualize each step of the process to write, edit, format and self-publish your book and later to make personal connections with your readers.

Daily visualization will really empower you to overcome self-limiting beliefs and habits like procrastination and motivate you to take the actions needed to reach for and achieve your goals.

3. Daily Journaling:

The definition of Journaling is: *a record of experiences, ideas, or reflections kept regularly for private use; an account of day-to-day events.*

Journaling is simply writing down the thoughts and ideas in your head for a few minutes each morning. I first learned to take journaling more seriously when I read *The Artist's Way* by Julia Cameron.

She shared how she wrote three handwritten pages of whatever came into her head each morning to clear the clutter in her mind. She called these pages *Morning Pages.*

Writing whatever comes to mind in the mornings gets

rid of thoughts that try to limit you and helps you pivot into thoughts of gratitude.

That shift out of clutter and a limiting mindset to gratefulness has been such a huge key to increasing my own creativity.

There's something freeing that begins to happen as you write down all the limiting thoughts that are clouding your mind.

When you take ten minutes to write down whatever is troubling you and shift it from your mind to the page, you can leave it on the page.

Next, write down a list of five details in your life that fill you with gratitude.

My list usually includes things like: *I'm grateful for an encouraging husband who supports me; I'm thankful for four kind and helpful young adult children; I'm grateful for the ability and freedom to write stories I love to share with readers who love my stories too.*

As you begin to write down what you're grateful for in your life each day, you'll begin to notice a shift to a greater capacity to receive more of what you want - more creativity, better relationships, finances, happiness into your life.

Writing out your list of gratitudes really helps and can change your mindset when you have an especially difficult day.

5 Benefits of Daily Journaling

A. Greater freedom from limiting thoughts:

As you write down your worries and things that trouble you in your notebook each morning, you'll find that getting those limiting thoughts out of your head and onto the page helps to free your mind. Once you have it on the page, I encourage you to leave it there.

B.Gain greater clarity: Writing in your journal helps you to write down what you're thinking, and by doing that you'll find you will be able to brainstorm and get more understanding and clarity. This new perspective will help you see things with more clarity and you'll often find the answers to problems that you were dealing with.

C.Expand your ideas: As you write, you'll notice more ideas come to mind. The wonderful aspect of writing in your journal is that you are totally free to write down whatever ideas come to mind and expand on them.

Your journal is private for only you to see, so you don't have to worry about needing to censor your words.

The great thing is you can always look back through your journal and see other ideas you've written down and it might jog your memory or give you more ideas on a book project.

D.Record Lessons Learned: When you journal everyday, you have the freedom to write down all the mistakes you've made and what you have learned from each one.

This helps to give you greater clarity and wisdom if

another situation comes up in the future where you could apply what you've learned.

E.Empower Your Growth: The nice thing about writing a daily journal, is that you can go back a year or two and reread your journal entries.

When you do read what you've written from years ago, you can see how much you've learned and grown. This is really empowering and can give you a big confidence boost.

The Productivity Learning Curve

So far if you've been following along in each chapter to this point, I hope you have taken a few minutes to write down the following:

• Your reason for writing your book
• How to clear your path from obstacles
• Your strategy and time frame to finish your book
• How you count the cost and commit to doing the hard work of writing your book.

Now you are ready to begin the productivity learning curve. What do I mean by that? This is simply about learning how to gradually increase how many words you write everyday in your work-in-progress.

The encouraging thing to remember is that every author, no matter how much they write now, began with a bank page. They faced the challenge of writing those first words of their story. They started at zero.

That's the kind of thing I like to remind myself when I

think of authors who inspire me like Debbie Macomber or Barbara Freethy.

If those authors, who have now written a lot of books, all started at zero and are doing very well today, then you can do this too.

I remember when I first started writing, I didn't count words or time how long I wrote(that might be one of the reasons why my first novel took over five years to write).

It was only as I wrote my second novel that I began to watch how many words I was writing, which was about 500 words a day most days. However, I still wasn't as consistent as I needed to be.

I was finally learning to be a more consistent writer as I wrote *Longing for Love* and Book One in this series of books for writers, *Write and Publish Your First Book*.

All you can do is start where you are. If all you can begin with is a 100 words a day or ten or fifteen minutes a day, then start there. *Rome wasn't built in a day.*

The most important thing to remember when writing to finish your book, is to be consistent. Write every day. If you've set a goal for 100 words, then decide that you will get those words written before you go to bed that night. Then, when you start to think 100 words is too easy, begin to write 150 or 200 words a day.

This is the learning curve that is a normal part of a writer's life. It's much like when you're learning anything for the first time.

Think back to when you learned to ride a bike. Maybe you started first by sitting on the bike to get your balance. Next you might have had a parent or older sibling hold the bike upright while you pushed the pedals. Then you started going a little faster.

At some point you finally were able to ride the bike on your own. All of that came from a step-by-step learning process.

Writing is no different. You will start to notice small growth in your confidence as you begin to be consistent in your writing and as you begin to increase how much you write everyday.

Set Up a Production Schedule for Your Writing

Now that you have learned how to take small steps to write more words regularly, you've already started to move from beginning writer to committed writer.

Bridging that gap is important if you want to finish your book by the deadline you have chosen.

The next step to take is to figure out how you can write enough words daily and weekly to finish your book by the deadline you have committed to.

As a reminder, you can refer back to Chapter Three on calculating your strategy, to learn how you can write, finish and market your book to reach a six month deadline.

So, if you decided you wanted to write two books a year, you would just repeat what you did in the first six months to reach your goal. Of course, there will always be things you can tweak in your writing or marketing, but that's normal.

I'm still learning how to create a production schedule that I can be consistent at doing on a regular basis. It is a big learning curve, but something that you can figure out.

. . .

Set Goals that Make You Happy and Align with Your Life

One last important thought on setting goals. It's really important to set goals that are in alignment with your life.

If you have a family, you'll want to double check that you've made time available to spend with them. If you have a day job, you'll need to add writing around that schedule.

It's important to think through what you hope to achieve with your writing. Ask yourself why do you write? Do you want to create more time in your life for your partner or children? Do you want to travel? Do you want to visit exotic places or meet new people?

Maybe your goal for writing, is so that you can write and work from home.

As writers, as much as we love to write, we hope for more from our writing than just producing books.

I write so that I can have more freedom. Freedom in time with my family, but also the freedom of location independence so that wherever I go I can still produce an income.

The thought of more freedom of time, creativity and location independence, makes me happy.

When you keep your reason for writing in front of you everyday it helps you to:

• Set goals that stretch me

• Set goals that excite and empower me

When you choose to write and finish your book - whether it's one book or many - it's important to set goals that inspire you to get up in the wee hours of the morning or motivate you to stay up later at night.

You don't want to only write, you want to live a great life too and the goals you set will mirror those desires.

Maybe right now you're saying, *okay I understand how to strategize and make room in my life to finish my book, but my real struggle is learning to focus as I write.*

This next chapter we will go through many helpful tips on how to uncover and get rid of those things that attempt to hinder our writing time and tips on how to concentrate when you sit down to write.

But, before you go to the next chapter, I encourage you to go through the questions and resources below to help you get clarity on how you can count the cost and commit.

Something to Try...

At the end of each chapter, I try offer some simple steps for you to begin to put into practice what you've learned.

I encourage you to take a few minutes to go answer the questions below and to check out the helpful resources.

I believe that going through these exercises, will help bring the clarity and inspiration to finish your book.

Questions to ask yourself:

• What are you willing to move around in your life so you can stick to your commitment to write?

• What results and benefits do you want to see when you finish your book? (examples: more income; fulfill your dream of writing; leaving a legacy, etc).

• Create your own vision board of the benefits you are passionate about when you finish your book(s).

• What are clear steps you need to take to achieve your goal? Plan your action plan for your writing for this coming week.

• Write out how you will use the 3 Daily Practices of 1)Daily Affirmations 2)Daily Visualization and 3)Daily Journaling to help you beat resistance in your writing.

Resources you might find helpful:

• *The Anti-Procrastination Mindset: The Simple Art of Finishing What You Start* by Harry Heijligers

• *The Miracle Morning for Writers: How to Build a Morning Ritual that Increases Your Impact and Your Income* by Hal Elrod, Steve Scott and Honoree Corder.

• Heinlein's 5 Simple Rules for Writers: https://www.createastoryyoulove.com/heinleins-5-simple-rules-for-writers/

• Podcast Interview on How to Start Simple Habits to Reach Your Writing Goals with bestselling NonFiction author Steve Scott: https://www.createastoryyoulove.com/stevescott

• *The Artist's Way* by Julia Cameron

• *Walking in this World* by Julia Cameron

Chapter Five

**oncentrate on Reaching Your Goals**

"Getting your work done is essential to making an impact.
You have to finish. Staying focused is how you do it."
  Jeff Goins

Many writers find it almost impossible to truly concentrate so they can get the words written.

Not only are there so many things that distract us throughout the day, but writers procrastinate a whole lot, trying to get past that stuck feeling to find that place where the words begin to easily flow.

When we face the blank page, or when we feel stuck writing a scene or chapter and we can't find the words, that's usually when we wish for creative flow.

We long for the words to flow quickly. We dream of losing ourselves in the story as we write our favourite scene or chapter.

The most important Key to getting your book written is to be able to replace distraction with concentration.

For most writers, this is easier said than done. This fight to break free from the continual distractions is something that plagues most people.

Turns out that people fight against their desires all day long according to a study led by psychologists Wilhelm Hofmann and Roy Baumeister in 2012. Dr. Baumeister summed up the details of this study in a book titled *Willpower,* which he co-wrote with John Tierney after the study was released.

It was found in this study that some of the most common distractions that people fight against are taking a break from hard work, checking email, checking social media, surfing the web, listening to music and watching television.

The study showed that the appeal of the Internet and Television were particularly difficult for most people to resist.

The more decisions you make, the more your brain becomes exhausted and your willpower goes out the window.

When this happens, you'll become too tired to resist your common diversions(checking email, social media, surfing the web, etc.) until you'll reach the point that you can no longer resist.

Soon you'll find yourself surfing the Internet or

sprawled out on the couch with a bag of chips, randomly flipping through television channels.

The real irony is that it's easier to become distracted, the more distracted you are.

The more you aren't focused on one thing at a time, the more problems you will have later on to finish one thing at a time.

So what will help us to break free from the addiction of distractions so we can focus on writing and finishing our books?

Begin to create intentional habits around your biggest desire. Since you're reading this book, more than likely your burning desire right now is to *finish your book*.

Let's dig a little deeper to uncover where your creative initiative comes from and how to activate that so you can really concentrate and finish your project.

Five Steps that Will Help Rewire and Refocus Your Creativity

"What other indicators does the Universe need to give to you, that you should be joyous at this stage of your life, that you deserve to chase good things in your life, that this is your time to start making new things happen, that is the time to enjoy your life?"
    Brendon Burchard

For years after I first started writing, always in the back of my mind, I had this constant feeling of being "stuck."

It was almost like an invisible force was holding me back from being able to fully focus on expressing my creativity.

This feeling of being held back was a huge source of frustration as I knew this was what hindered my progress in writing and finishing more books.

I was looking through my old journals from a few years ago, reading through some notes I wrote on the struggles of my writing journey:

> "I feel so frustrated with myself and my lack of writing. Somehow I need to break down what's holding me back from writing these books faster. Sometimes I feel so overwhelmed with all the details involved with writing, but that's not the biggest problem that holds me back. Every time I sit down to write there is this massive fear of failure and self-doubt that weighs on me, a feeling that whatever I write won't be good enough. I want to understand the reason for it and then do whatever it takes to get rid of it."

You can probably tell by the journal entry above that I knew I needed to take the initiative to find the answers necessary to break my creativity free from its cage.

It was only after deciding to read books, blogposts and listen to videos that I came across some game changing inspiration and advice from High Performance Coach, Brendon Burchard.

I learned that...

"Your initiative flows from your intentions and determines where you're going in life."

However, I would like to share with you what I've learned and how it has led to my own "aha" moment and breakthrough in my writing. I hope this will help you in some way as well.

Before we dive deep into this topic, I want to add a disclaimer: I am not a medical doctor, psychologist, neuroscientist, counsellor or therapist of any kind and that if you feel you want professional help in this area please consult a professional.

I always wondered how the brain took information in and how sometimes situations in our life we processed as safe or unsafe.

I also wanted to understand the connection between the information we take in and whether it triggers something in us to choose to take action or not.

What I learned was really eye-opening. Basically our brain is a complex spider web of intricate wiring and has an interconnectivity that is phenomenal.

Which is why some things that happened in our childhood, for example, can show up when we're adults and cause us to take action or not take action depending on how we interpreted different events and how we labelled ourselves because of it.

I realized this is part of my own journey from childhood to adulthood and I've been learning how to be more aware of how I am interpreting different events or situations so that I don't label myself incorrectly and then hinder or stop my ability to take action on my writing.

As I share these five levels of how our brains process information, realize this is just touching the surface and there is so much more to know about how our mind processes things.

But I really think this is helpful to be aware of, especially if you feel like your own writing has been hindered either through procrastination, perfectionism or any other kind of resistance.

5 Levels of How our Mind Processes Information [Simplified]

Understanding or being very aware of our own thoughts and feelings and how we are interpreting different events and situations really does affect our ability to be either hindered or to have freedom in our creativity.

After many years of feeling stuck in my own writing, I finally realized one of the hindrances to my own creativity has been how I have interpreted and applied some situations to my own identity. I'll explain more as you read on.

First, I thought it would be helpful to explain these five levels to give an idea of how our mind processes information (for more books and resources on this topic, please look at the resources at the end of this chapter).

How Our Mind Receives Information and Next Steps that Move Us Toward Taking Action:

Below is a simple, straightforward route that our minds take from receiving information to taking action. Of course, our brains are not as simplified as this. Our minds are a spider web of interconnectedness and intelligence that neuroscientists tell us they still don't understand.

However, since it was through learning these five simple levels of how our mind works that gave me a breakthrough to understand how to rewire my own creative process, that's how I'll share this process below.

1. Our minds receive information.

As we go throughout our regular lives, information comes into our brain. We might be working, studying or having conversations with our family or friends.

At this point, information that enters our minds is about details like: what we're learning; how people treat us; how people perceive us, and the cause and effect of events, and more.

2. Our minds Interpret the Information.

From the point of the information entering our minds, that information immediately goes to interpretation.

It's a really fast, reactive process. This is when we make a snap judgement about something as to whether we like it or don't like it.

This means we have a fast reaction and ask ourselves whether this is: *safe or unsafe; familiar or unfamiliar; good or bad; certain or uncertain; recognize it or don't recognize it.*

This is also when our biases come into play. We either interpret the information as good or bad.

This is done at the unconscious level in our minds and is usually a snap judgement.

. . .

3.Our minds apply the Interpretation to our Identity.

Again our minds move quickly from interpreting the information, to applying this to our identity.

When we apply our interpretation of the event to our identity, we ask questions like: *What does this mean to me? What does this say about me? How does this apply to me?*

How we label things here and label ourselves is where we can really change our lives forever. It's at this turning point that we need to be very aware of our own thoughts and feelings and how we describe ourselves.

4.Our minds then set an Intention.

After we've observed our thoughts and have asked questions about how we feel this applies to our identity, the next thing our mind does is set an intention.

What this means, is that *we decide from our answers in the interpretation and identity steps, whether we will choose intentions that have the potential to either hinder or advance our progress.*

In the intention step we ask questions like: *what do I want to do with this information? What am I going to do in the future because of this? What is my next action to take from this?*

How you answer these questions can put you either in self-protective mode or keep you open to new possibilities.

5.Our minds then set our initiative.

From the intention we set in the above steps, flows all our initiative. The spark we feel to take action is from ambition and expectancy.

In this last step, we ask questions like: *what do you really want to do in the world? What goals are you going after? How are you really showing up?*

Most people don't understand where their initiative - their motivation to take action - comes from. I didn't understand this either, which is why learning these steps has been so helpful.

Some Key Takeaways and Lessons Learned

As you read the above five steps, I hope the process the mind goes through made sense for your own journey.

To help clarify these steps, I wanted to share what I learned from my own journey and how it has affected my identity, ability to concentrate and freedom to take focused creative action.

My biggest hope is that by being vulnerable and sharing my own journey from both positive and negative aspects, it will help you find a breakthrough in your writing journey.

A Glimpse into Unravelling What Has Hindered my own Mindset:

Information received:

• *Positive:* Lessons learned from a young age, was to be willing to try new things, because that's how you understand what you're good at and how you get better at different life skills.

• *Negative:* Lessons learned early on that when I shared too freely(spoken or written), it caused pain of some kind in the form of rejection, criticism or judgement.

Interpretation applied:

• *Positive:* Lessons learned and my interpretation was that sometimes it's good to put yourself out there to try new things because that's how you learn and grow.

• *Negative:* Lessons Learned and my interpretation of the pain of rejection and criticism, was that I feel bad about myself.

Identity adjusted:

• *Positive:* Lessons learned and the identity that I embraced was that I feel more like I belong when I get rewarded for trying new things.

• *Negative:* Lessons learned and the identity I embraced from the pain of rejection and feeling bad about myself, is that in some areas I can never be safe again.

Intention practiced:

• *Positive:* Lessons learned and the intention that I put into practice was in the future I would try new things and grow my skills.

• *Negative:* Lessons learned and the intention that I put into practice from my conclusion that in some areas I would never be safe again, was in the future to never put myself in a position to share who I really am(spoken or written) because those people hurt my feelings and caused so much pain.

Initiative decided:

• *Positive:* Lessons learned and the initiative decided

for future action, was to excel in music and to continue to read and learn new things.

• *Negative*: Lessons learned and the initiative decided from not feeling safe, was that the goals I would chase would be those that would keep me safe and as well protected as I could be from rejection or criticism.

Whew! That was really hard to write. I felt nervous just writing the list above, because I feel like I'm unravelling the deep, dark struggles of my creative soul.

However, I felt compelled to share a little about the war that's been going on in my head, especially as it relates to freeing my creativity onto the page.

As you read the lessons learned above, maybe one or two ideas resonated or shed light on some areas in your own writing journey.

Maybe you too have realized that at some point in your life, you chose self-protection. I chose to protect myself too.

I only realized much later, that by doing that I had not only blocked out one of the things I desired most(connection with others), but I had also caused a block in my own creativity by setting up so many walls of self-protection.

My big *aha moment,* was when I realized I had told myself the story that I am just protecting myself from pain.

But the truth was, I was just scared to let myself be free and vulnerable again because I didn't want to be hurt once again.

As I've become aware of how the mind works a little more, I've chosen to observe how and when I have a tendency to put negative labels on myself, thereby blocking my creativity.

The lesson learned here is to observe how we label our identity and intentions carefully, because out of intentions flow all of our initiative.

It's only when our identity and intentions are free to flow unhindered, that we are freed up to take the action we really want to take, like writing and finishing a book.

The takeaway, is to ask yourself if you are taking the action you want to take everyday throughout the week.

If you find your writing has stalled out in some way, simply ask yourself what happened earlier that week that might have hindered your progress.

Here's an example:

• On Monday there was something you couldn't figure out either in a project at work or in your writing(information received).

• Perhaps, you believed this project was doomed to fail(your interpretation).

• Next, you told yourself that what this said about you was that *I'm going to be a failure again(your identity)*.

• In the end, you decided *I shouldn't even try anymore(your intention)*.

• So finally, you decided to give up and watch Netflix instead(your initiative).

So if you find yourself dealing with a ton of self-doubt or limiting beliefs, ask yourself what happened earlier that day or that week.

You might find the answer to this question sheds some light on where the self-doubt began in the first place.

Next, reverse the script that hindered you in each of the above five steps and you'll begin to rewire your mindset.

Ideas on how to reverse the script from the above example:

• Monday there was something you couldn't figure out in a project at work or in your writing(information received).

• Perhaps, you believed this project would either fail or succeed depending on your next steps(your interpretation).

• Next, you told yourself that what this said about you, was that *I am confident that there is some way to figure this out either by researching, asking a mentor and/or by learning and working at it(your identity).*

• In the end, you decided *I will keep trying and work on this until somehow I figure out a solution(your intention).*

• Finally, you decided *I won't give up. I will take action everyday until I've got this figured out(your initiative).*

As you read this last example on reversing the script, I hope it has given you a glimpse into how you can make a shift in your own process from information to initiative.

If you use this five step process as a tool, it can help you to observe what's going on and you'll be able to shake things up so you can accelerate your own writing.

Sometimes Fear Can Be A Writer's Biggest Distraction. How to Use it to Transform Your Writing.

I believe that fear can be a writer's biggest distraction, taking us off course or procrastinating on where our focus should really be —like finishing that book.

Fear has the ability to speak so loudly in our subconscious or conscious mind that we suddenly decide we need to do whatever it takes to get fear's nagging voice out of our heads.

Sometimes this is when we distract ourselves by checking social media, email or doing some other kind of busy work.

Maybe this isn't true for every writer, but it was (and is) certainly true for me.

When I first started writing, it was fear of failure and fear of sharing my work with others that often caused me to procrastinate on my writing. Later, it was the fear of expectations and fear of being found out as not a 'real' writer.

As I've continued to write, I've realized that fear is an essential part of every writer's life.

With every interview I've had with bestselling authors, each one of them has had to deal with fear in one way or another. At first, this surprised me, but the more I listened to how fear tried to stop them, and what they did to keep writing anyway, I realized this was common.

I learned that all writers face fears, and that it's really an essential part of writing.

In some way, you should seek out that which you fear most as that's where your soul's real transformation lies. But this only works well, if you can train your fear — meaning that you: accept your fear; name your fear, and take action in spite of the fear.

When many of my own mentors, successful authors in the indie author community, shared how they took action to write their books anyway as fears tried to hinder them, I learned an important lesson: ***creative action buries fear.***

As I've taken action to write my story in spite of huge fears, I've learned that creative action really does cause fear to take a backseat to the creative process.

When I choose every day to make my regular writing practice as low resistance and as simple as possible, then it seems like fear doesn't speak so loudly in my ear.

I've learned that combining positive daily practices, with tiny habits of writing (see chapter two), alongside timed writing sessions has helped me to tame the voice of fear so I can write with more freedom.

Flip the Script so Your Creative Ideas Flow Freely

When we flip the script of what we tell ourselves in all five of these levels to the positive, it helps unlock our creativity.

Then, what we tell ourselves will change from unbelief to belief in our ability to write and tell our story.

In my own journey, it was when I chose to see the redemptive value in the different fears and self-doubt that caused resistance in the past, that I began a shift in perspective.

I encourage you to give it try, you might be surprised at the positive results and freedom of creativity this brings you.

Try using the simple tools of daily affirmations, visualization and journaling to help shift you towards positive self-affirmations and confidence building(and if you want tips on how to do that, please refer back to chapter four).

The very act of trying something new brings about changes in the way you see yourself. When you choose not to do what you've always done, and decide rather to embrace the new, you empower yourself to explore and take action on your writing dreams.

However, this shift to greater freedom in your creative ideas and your writing won't happen overnight.

This is a process that takes a daily practice of affirming positive traits of who you are becoming and to set a positive conscious intention to give yourself permission to believe and take action on your dreams.

Do Whatever You Must to Protect Your Focus

Since it's during concentrated times when you do things like write or accomplish other tasks, you need to do whatever it takes to protect your focus.

The things you get done during the day - whether it's with your day job or with your writing - are accomplished during the windows of time that you are focused on that particular task.

We all have interruptions. However the number and type of interruptions are greater now than they've ever been.

I remember back in the 1980s and early 1990s when we didn't have cell phones or computers and all the myriad of distractions that exist now. It seemed like it was a little easier to concentrate on a task then.

Most of us nowadays get bombarded with email, Facebook and other social media notifications constantly.I notice that my concentration starts to slip the more I allow these loops to open.

For example: If I see an interesting conversation on Facebook, or Twitter, I find it leaves a residual effect on my mind when I start writing. This unwanted debris sticks to the edges of my mind, surfacing just when I'm trying to get into the story.

Here's what I've noticed among writers that I've talked to. When we are constantly splitting our attention between too many things - whether it's social media, email or chasing the next shiny object - we feel busy, but in all honesty we aren't getting much writing done.

So, I've committed myself to learn how to limit the type of distractions that get in the way of writing.

I've learned a little secret that helps me and maybe it'll help you too.

I've noticed if I don't open Facebook or other social media or email loops until after I've had my focused writing time, my level of productivity skyrockets.

I want to encourage you to look at what's going on in your everyday life.

Ask yourself a few questions and answer them honestly: How is your focus? How often are you getting that dopamine hit from checking social media? Could you prune the amount of time spent on social media or email? If you were to minimize that time, would you be able to focus better and get more writing done?

I suspect that if you give it try, you'll find that your levels of concentration go up and that the quality and quantity of the work you do will soon follow.

Add Routines and Habits Around Your Work

A key strategy to help you limit the amount of everyday distractions is to develop routines and habits around your work.

When you have a habit setup in your life, it moves you beyond the place of having good intentions to write your book to the point where you've designed your life in such a way that writing has become a regular part of your life.

When you have setup smart routines, like a set time and a quiet location where you write each day, it will require less willpower to begin your new writing habit.

As you have created space to write, this new routine will help you be successful in getting into the deep flow of writing your book more often.

Some Ways to Create Space For Focused Writing

To add this new writing routine into your life means you need to figure out a way that is best for your own lifestyle.

No two writers are the same. What each writer needs and can make work in their lives will be different than another.

That's why I thought it would be helpful to list a few ideas on how you can set up a writing habit in your life.

There are many different ways to find the space for concentrated writing time in your life, but in this book I thought I'd mention three ideas. Maybe one of these ideas will work for you.

1. Write using the Sprint method.

This is one way of creating space to write that works if it works better for you to write within a prolonged period of time, like one or two weeks, where you can focus primarily on writing.

Sometimes this works, if you can put off for a week or two some of your other tasks and distractions. You would also need to talk to your family or friends and explain that you want focused writing time during this time period.

For some writers, this type of deep concentrated work would produce extreme productivity and they would likely get quite a lot of words written during a focused writing sprint.

2. Write using the Chain Method.

The Chain Method can be described as making the

choice to keep a daily writing practice for an extended period of time, so you don't break the chain.

This method of writing was made popular by Jerry Seinfeld as he explained to a young writer and comic Brad Isaac, how to be a better comic(*look in the resources at the end of the chapter to read this article on LifeHacker*).

Seinfeld explained that "the way to be a better comic was to create better jokes." He went on to say that "the way to create better jokes was to write every day."

Seinfeld said the technique he used to keep up this routine was to put a calendar on his wall. Everyday he writes a joke, he crosses out the date on the calendar with a big red X.

"After a few days you'll have a chain," Seinfeld explained. "Just keep at it and the chain will grow longer every day. You'll like seeing that chain, especially when you get a few weeks under your belt. Your only job next is to not break the chain. Don't break the chain."

If you can build daily writing practice into your schedule, do it. A simple regular writing habit, is one of the easiest ways to consistently start focused time-blocks of writing.

You will soon find yourself improving by leaps and bounds, and as a bonus, you'll finish more books!

3.Writing using the Shift Method.

The shift method of writing is simply that you shift into deep work mode anytime you have a free moment to write.

When you write in this way, you work writing around your day job and your family's schedule and basically train yourself to shift into writing mode whenever you have a few minutes free to write.

The ability to switch your mind from shallow to deep concentrated writing takes a little bit of practice. It's not something that comes naturally, but you can train yourself to make the switch from your regular daily schedule to grab ten minutes of writing time when it becomes available.

This is a method that I want to learn to get better at doing. I have written often in the lineup to get my groceries, but I would like to train myself to write whenever I get a chance.

But for now, I've chosen to write using the Chain method. There are many other ways that you can experiment with to find concentrated time to write, but I hope the above examples have helped give you ideas to get started.

I hope you were able to figure out which method will work best for you so you can ease yourself into concentrated writing mode.

Setup Your Sacred Writing Space

"Nobody cares much whether you write or not. You just have to do it." *Natalie Goldberg, Writing Down the Bones*

As I've observed and learned from successful authors, one of the key disciplines that has propelled them faster and further toward their goals, is a consistent writing practice.

You need to create a steady writing habit that works for you. I recommend writing at least a little, every day. When I first started writing, I would write whenever the mood struck me, and that didn't work so well.

I didn't get a lot of words written on my novel at the time. It wasn't until I decided to write a little everyday - even if it was only for ten minutes - that I began to make some steady progress on my book.

To empower yourself to write and finish your book, it's important to create a time and a place where you can get it done.

When all is said and done, how much time it takes for you to write your book will come down to the choices you make in your everyday life, your personality and how compelling your reason is for you to get your book into the world.

Make a plan that works for you and stick to it.

Define Your Own Writing Time and Space

Defining a space that you use for writing is important.

This isn't only about a physical space, but this also about a time and place that your mind attaches to that says *this is where I write.*

Your writing space could be at home, a coffee shop or any other place where you are able to concentrate on your writing.

If you only have one computer and it's a desktop then

it may not be possible to go anywhere else. But you can still make a writing space that's all your own.

If it's the same computer you do everything else on, then you can always block yourself from browsing through websites and social media. I like using an app called Freedom to block the Internet.

I've created a simple writing space of my own at home. I write in my own corner desk in my upstairs bedroom. It's the space I have where it's quiet and when the door is closed, most of the time I won't be interrupted.

I like writing in early mornings, so usually I get going by 5:30am. The quiet of the morning is peaceful and invites deep thoughts, which is why I love to write in the early morning hours.

If you have your family nearby when you write, let them know you'll be writing for a certain amount of time and that you can't be interrupted during that time. Then close the door.

That's what I've done, and it really works well. My family now understands my need to write and later in the day I make time for them too.

If you need to write early mornings or after everyone has gone to bed, then do whatever works best for you. It's important that however you find your space to write, that you must get rid of all distractions.

In my own writing journey, I've noticed that distractions are devastating to creative flow. Every time I check a text message, check email or talk to someone in my family, it takes me around fifteen minutes to get back into the writing from where I left off.

So, really try to find a writing space even if it's only for fifteen minutes at a time to start with. You'll be surprised at how much you can get done in short bursts like that.

That's how I'm writing this book right now. I write in twenty-five minute time blocks with a five minute break in between each writing block. I do two in a row and then I take a fifteen minute break before I start all over again.

I encourage you to make a commitment to yourself that you will write for a certain amount of time everyday. And if it helps you, make it a priority to do the hard stuff in your day first, like writing.

When I started my day with writing, it dramatically changed my ability to focus and I was able to get more words written every day. This is a huge confidence boost!

Next, after you've found the time and space where you can concentrate to write each day, it's important to take the time to write out what this chapter or scene is about before you sit down to write it.

This is something that I didn't clue into as important when I first started writing. *Read on, and I'll explain more.*

Know What You Are Writing Before You Write It

When I began my first novel, I only had a vague idea of what I was writing.

I started writing it without any sort of outline, I just tried working from the ideas in my head. A movie played in my head in bits and pieces while I wrote; that's all I needed, right?

I got this part(along with many others) wrong.

I honestly believe that was one of the reasons it took

me much longer to write that first novel. Everything was so vague and the storyline was somewhat muddled, that I didn't really know where it was going to go next.

So what did I do? I went in the complete opposite direction for the second novel in that series. I not only had a ten page outline, but I actually hired an editor to edit my outline.

Okay, so that might have been overkill, I don't know. The good news is that I ended up finding a happy balance between writing from a vague idea and edited outline that worked for me.

The simple truth is that what works for one writer won't necessarily work for the next writer. We're all different in the way we write.

However, whether you write from an outline or not, the suggestion I would submit to you, dear writer, is to know what you are writing before you write it.

Seriously. This will not only save you time, but will increase your ability to concentrate by a factor of ten.

I'm sure that I would have at least cut the time in half from my first novel if I would have taken the time to write down scenes and chapters.

A tip here that might help to uncover the mystery of your story: *Grab a notebook and a pen and begin to scribble down what your upcoming scenes are in the book you're writing.*

Even if all you write is a paragraph or two, that's okay. Just write down in short sentences the idea you have for the next scene. You'll be amazed at how much this will help you.

(*Just a note: if you don't want to use a notebook, try*

a whiteboard. I used a whiteboard to jot down notes for this book, and it was pure magic as it helped to untangle my thought process).

Rachel Aaron, in her helpful book for storytellers, *2K to 10K*(see resources at the end of the chapter), shares how she also writes down a quick description of the scene she is planning to write that day. She spends five minutes writing out the description and then she begins to write.

I encourage you to try this. I can testify that doing this one simple thing has helped me to concentrate better and write with more confidence.

Now that we've learned how to set up your space for writing, we're ready to talk about the best part of the writing process: *finding your creative flow.*

Finding Your Creative Flow

> "To build your working life around the experience of flow produced by deep work is a proven path to deep satisfaction."
>
> *Cal Newport* in his book: *"Deep Work"*

After you have put in place positive daily practices, created your writing space and you've written down a description of your next scene, you're ready for the next step.

Now you're ready to begin writing your story. However maybe you are staring at the blank page a little longer as you try to figure out where to begin.

If you experience this feeling of *how do I begin*, I want to share with you something that has helped me.

When I face the blank page and procrastinate and am unsure where to begin, I take that to mean that I need to take another look at the scene or dig deeper into the back-story of the main character's story. Once more, I write those details down until I get to the place where I am fully engaged and enjoying the story and have a good idea of where it's going once more.

Ask a bunch of questions of your character and world, to dive deeper into that scene you're about to write. It'll help you get a clear picture of where your story is going.

Next, as you begin to write your story again, and your story is now headed down the right path, you'll find a natural enthusiasm and enjoyment comes back to your writing.

It's a wonderful feeling to be happy and peaceful when you are writing. Rather than feeling like writing your book is a drudgery, telling your story should be fun and bring an amazing sense of contentment and fulfillment.

Part of the writing process is getting to that place of joy in your storytelling.

Most of us long for the words to flow quickly. We dream of losing ourselves in that favorite scene or chapter. We want that feeling of when we're itching to keep writing and never stop until the end. The way to get there, is to enter creative flow with your writing.

You might be asking, what is creative flow?

In Mihaly Csikszentmihalyi's classic book on *Creativity: Flow and the Psychology of Discovery and Invention*, he shares his discoveries as he interviewed many rock climbers, dances, composers and other creative people and how they described the experience of being in creative flow:

> *"It was clear from talking to them that what kept them motivated was the quality of experience they felt when they were involved with the activity. This feeling didn't come when they were relaxing, when they were taking drugs or alcohol... rather it often involved painful, risky, difficult activities that stretched the person's capacity and involved and element of novelty and discovery. This optimal experience is what I have called flow, because many of the respondents described the feeling when things were going well as an almost automatic, effortless, yet highly focused state of consciousness."*

In simple terms: creative flow is a state you reach when you are absorbed in a project or when you are totally immersed in your creative project.

You'll know you're in creative flow when...

- You lose track of time.
- You forget about others and basically the world around you.
- You feel happier, have more clarity and focused direction.
- You have increased imagination and productivity.

Creative Flow is one of the most important keys to achieving your writing goals.

This type of focused, deep work, is what helps you get books written and published.

It's by losing ourselves in important and challenging tasks, that helps writers to get our most memorable and profitable projects written and out into the world.

What happens when writers get into creative flow...

When you get into that place where you really are deep into your story and unconscious of the world around you, it is a wonderful feeling.

From my own experience of creative flow, I've found that the fear of failure seems to fade away(at least for the few minutes I'm in flow). This is truly an enjoyable feeling.

I've discovered in my own writing, that each of the factors listed below, happen when we get into a writing flow. This creative flow makes writing the story an experience that is fun and enjoyable.

1.Having clear goals for each step, makes the work is enjoyable.

When you know the next step to take in the process, you are more confident and you know how to proceed moment by moment.

2.Distractions fade away and your focus increases.

As you are in creative flow, you are only aware of what you are focused on working on in the moment. To get into flow, you are in intense concentration which lets the fear and anxiety slip away from the forefront of your mind.

3.You feel like your abilities are an even match with the actions you take.

This is true in writing, when we're in flow we often just write and it feels sometimes like the story is telling itself.

4.You are aware of how well you are doing when you're creative flow.

This is a helpful part of being in the state of flow. You have immediate feedback on your work and it helps you to understand how well you're doing.

5.Your concentration is focused on your actions in the moment.

In most of our usual everyday experiences, we're doing one task while thinking about something else. In flow state, your actions and awareness become fused together. This is helped by your clarity of goals and constantly being aware of how well you're doing.

6.Intense concentration in the moment frees you from distractions worry and fear.

When you are completely absorbed in creative flow, generally you are only aware of the here and now. You are focused and deeply immersed in your story, which takes away the usual fears that cause anxiety, distraction and worry.

7.Your self-consciousness fades away.

The burden of self-awareness and worrying about what others think of us disappears when you are in flow. When you are super focused on writing your story, you are too involved in what you are doing in the moment to care about protecting your ego.

8. You lose track of time.

When you are fully engaged in flow, hours can pass by without you realizing it.

All of the above positive results are from getting into creative flow as you begin writing. I've experienced all of these myself when I get "in the zone" of writing a story. That's why it not only feels wonderful but is super helpful to do whatever you can to achieve this flow state when you begin writing.

I encourage you to do what you can to set up your writing space so that you are free from distractions and interruptions so that you can get into your own creative flow. You will be so glad you did.

As I continued to learn more about creative flow, I discovered that it's important for those in creative activities like writing to learn how to develop personal objectivity around your own writing.

In Mihaly Csikszentmihalyi's book, he shares...

"(Flow is possible when eight conditions are met, one of which...) occurs when we confront tasks we have the chance of completing. The task undertaken has clear goals and provides immediate feedback... *In some creative activities, where goals are not clearly set in advance, a person must develop a strong personal sense of what she intends to do. The artist might not have a visual* image of what the finished painting should look like, but when the picture has progressed to a certain point, she should know whether this is what she wanted to achieve or not. And a painter who enjoys painting must have internalized criteria for "good" or "bad" so that after each brush stroke she can say: "Yes, this works; no, this doesn't." Without such internal guidelines, it is impossible to experience flow."

Mihaly Csikszentmihalyi, Creativity: Flow and the Psychology of Discovery and Invention

When I read this, it was an epiphany for me. I hadn't realized the importance of developing personal objectivity around my own writing, until I read the above book about the conditions around achieving creative flow.

Being objective about your work is a key skill to develop in order to reap the full benefit of creative flow.

In other words, this is not only about turning off your inner critic as you write.

Getting into creative flow also means that as you are in the middle of tackling your writing project, that you, the author, have a sense of whether you are moving toward your vision of the book or not.

You sense internally whether you are reaching the goals you have set for this particular book.

This is important. You, as the author and original idea creator, decide when your book is actually finished.

Yes it's important to have your book edited after you have finished the first draft. But, while you are writing that first draft, if you seek out external validation, it will shatter your creative flow.

So first finish writing your book, then get feedback. Or, as Stephen King succinctly puts it, "write with the door closed."

As you work on finishing your book, even if it's your very first book, it's so important to develop belief in yourself and faith in your work.

Believe in Yourself and Have Faith in Your Work

Sometimes one of the most difficult aspects of writing a story is believing in yourself enough to write the story that you love.

Begin by nurturing and respecting your own vision of the world. This unique offering you give to others through your writing is the treasure you bring to the table.

This is that part of you that makes you special, and as in all creative businesses, that uniqueness you offer is the most valuable thing you own.

It's not easy to uncover your own vision. But, you'll find your vision as you continue to write and as you search for the pearls of wisdom and shiny gold nuggets among words you produce.

This might take a few years of writing to dig deep enough to discover the truth in you that wants to be found.

As you keep crafting words and finishing books, this will help you narrow down what you are really trying to say.

Understanding your unique storytelling ability is one of the most important things you can do as a writer.

When others offer suggestions for you to change your

story, it's important that you know the heart of what you're trying to say, so you keep the true essence of that.

It's when you have a deep understanding of what your true story is, that you'll be able to say: *yes, that's a good idea, or I appreciate your thoughts on this, but that doesn't fit with what I'm trying to say here, so I'll keep the story the way it was written.*

I encourage you to be willing to simply write your first draft imperfectly. Have faith in the process. Believe that the story is in you and it wants to come out. You can always fix the words later.

In an interview with NY Times bestselling author Joanna Penn, she shares tips on how writers can learn to trust emergence of their story(see the resources at the end of this chapter for a link to this interview).

Have faith in yourself and your ability to grow and learn as a writer and a storyteller. As you continue to put in the effort to write, and as you keep learning, you will grow in greater confidence in your writing.

You can write your story. So just do it.

In the next chapter, we'll talk about how to charge up and level up as a writer so you can continue to grow into the writer you want to be.

Something to Try...

At the end of each chapter I try offer some simple steps for you to begin to put into practice what you've learned.

I encourage you to take a few minutes to go answer the questions below and to check out the helpful resources.

I believe that going through these exercises, will help bring the clarity and inspiration to finish your book.

Questions to ask yourself:

• What distractions pull you away from writing?

• In what ways have you blocked your intention to write? (examples are: negative labels; self-protection; false identity, etc).

• How can you flip the script so you give yourself a positive identity and so that your ideas flow freely?

• How have you created time and space for your writing?

• What are some ways you can trust the emergence of your story as you are writing?

Resources you might find helpful:

• *Willpower: Rediscovering the Greatest Human Strength* by Dr. Roy F. Baumeister and John Tierney

• Article and Video on How the Mind Works and how it relates to taking action by High Performance Coach, Brendon Burchard - https://www.createastoryyoulove. com/brendonburchard

• Article on Jerry Seinfeld's Chain Method as told by Brad Isaac: www.lifehacker.com/jerryseinfeld

• *2K to 10K: Writing Faster, Writing Better, and Writing More of What You Love* by Rachel Aaron

• *You Are A Writer (So Start Acting Like One)* by Jeff Goins

• *On Writing: A Memoir of the Craft* by Stephen King

- *Write Down the Bones* by Natalie Goldberg
- *Deep Work: Rules for Focused Success in a Distracted World* by Cal Newport
- *Creativity: Flow and the Psychology of Discovery and Invention* by Mihaly Csikszentmihalyi
- How you can learn to trust story emergence – an interview with NY Times bestselling author Joanna Penn: www.createastoryyoulove.com/joannapenn

Chapter Six

Charge Up & Level Up

"When we're living as amateurs, we're running away from our calling - meaning our work, our destiny, the obligation to become our truest and highest selves."
  Steven Pressfield, Turning Pro

It's one thing to learn writing practices that help you to finish your book.

But, it's another thing to embrace the regular habit of being fully present, pushing past challenges and enthusiastically creating your own journey as a writer.

That's why this chapter is about learning how to charge up and level up as a writer.

But what does it mean to charge up? Well in the

context of this chapter it seems appropriate that the word *charge* has several meanings, which you can read about below.

The Collins Dictionary defines the word *charge* as: *to command; to fill or suffuse with feeling emotion; to aim in position ready for use; to load or fill to capacity; to saturate one substance with another; to give as a task or duty; to attack vigorously or move forward as if attacking.*

Simply put, a charged up writer, is learning to be fully engaged in defining your writer's journey exactly as you want it to look.

Someone who is living charged up, is less about being trapped in old ruts or familiar mindsets or skill sets and more about being engaged in the present and stretching their abilities.

It's more about doing what's right and what's meaningful to them. It's more about learning to enjoy the writing journey, to push past the obstacles that land in your way and continuing to positively shape and reinvent their present and future.

The important phrase here is that you are *learning to live charged up in your writing journey.*

Please, don't feel like this is something that happens in one day. And I hope you don't feel discouraged if you are new to this writing thing.

Learning to live charged up is a constant learning process for me.

Just like any other writer, I have to choose to commit daily to steady growth in my writing practice, my mindset and my skills in all areas of my author business.

I remember when I first started writing, I felt excitement but also fear, intimidation and discouragement as I wondered how I would ever write even one book, never mind the many books I wanted to get out into the world.

I was so discouraged and overwhelmed as I began to realize all the steps I needed to learn. I didn't know how to get an editor, didn't know how to format a book and I really didn't know how to upload an ebook to digital retailers like Amazon, Kobo and others.

Basically, I didn't know a thing about writing. All I had going for me, was the spark of a story idea in my head.

I was starting at zero.

As I continued to read blogposts and listened to podcast interviews of bestselling authors and heard their stories, I realized that every writer starts at the very beginning. I wasn't alone in this.

Just knowing that, brought the smidgeon of hope I needed to take the next step.

You can do the same.

Everybody Starts at the Beginning...

Every writer starts at zero. We aren't born knowing how to write stories. We must learn how to tell stories... and we must keep learning if we want to succeed at becoming the author we want to be.

As writers, each one of us starts at zero and we learn and grow from there.

Honestly, sometimes the biggest problem that we face as writers is comparing ourselves to authors that we believe are overnight successes.

(*Hint: It's not overnight. More often than not the authors we admire, have been writing for a lot longer than we think*).

If you are struggling with comparing yourself with other more successful authors that you admire, there is a way to prevent yourself from doing that.

Give yourself permission to be not-so-good at writing and all things related to getting your book into the hands of readers.

Let yourself begin at *zero* and accept the truth of where you are at right now.

Something that might help is to look at your writing like a journey through school, from Kindergarten all the way through High School.

When you think of learning to write like a journey through school, it becomes much easier to accept limitations. When you think of it this way, it'll be easier to accept that anything you're working on right now will be the work of an amateur.

It's not a fault to admit that you are beginner. The fault lies in knowing you're a beginner and expecting yourself immediately to become a master.

Making the leap from Grade one to Grade twelve in a week's time just doesn't happen whether it's in school or writing. First you learn from the beginning and you gradually go to third, fourth and fifth grade and higher.

It takes a lot of effort and thousands of hours at the writing craft.

If you're a newbie writer right now who is around grade two in your writing journey, it's okay.

Sometimes when you're new to writing you'll have

readers telling you they were disappointed when they read your book, but try not to let it get to you. Every writer goes through terrible reviews. Just don't give up as you wade through the mud and mire of the ups and downs of your writing journey.

This was my experience. Sadly, I gave up writing when I was in elementary school, and didn't get back to it until my children were learning to write stories in grade school. I had told myself there was no way I could do this. I told myself that there was no way I could ever make money at writing.

When I first started following successful self-published authors in 2011 and 2012, that's when I had a flash of insight.

I realized from their success stories of starting at zero and committing to the learning process, that I could do that too.

One thing I knew could do, was be committed to learning. Learning new things was something I was confident I could do, as that was something ingrained in me from a young age.

Listening to stories of successful authors increased my awareness that these writers were normal people just like me.

They were people who were passionate about writing stories who had also started as beginners. This realization made me ask myself, what would happen if I jumped in right now and chose to commit to writing again?

I realized that what would make the difference between whether I failed or succeeded would be based on if I quit writing entirely. This time I desperately wanted to write the stories in my heart. I was passionate to succeed.

When I got back on the horse, I realized I was maybe in second grade in my writing, but that was okay. I decided I would keep learning until I got better and increased my writing craft until my books were better. But this was okay, I was ready to do this.

I hope you choose to stick to it. I hope you choose to write your book, no matter if you're a beginner.

All writers start at the beginning, so no matter where you're at, please believe you can do this.

You can write and finish your book.

How to Close the Gap Between Beginner and Master Artist

For many writers, it's the vision we have in our imaginations - the books we want to write - that gets us into this writing game in the first place.

Many times books we envision, are memorable memoirs, educational and inspirational nonfiction books or "un-put-down-able" novels.

It's an awesome thing to conceive of how we want our book or books to take shape.

I remember being disappointed by the huge gap that existed between the words I wrote in my first novel to the great masterpiece I had imagined in my mind.

It was my taste, the ideas that formed my vision that were battling with my beginning storytelling skills.

This is the dilemma every artist faces as they work to close the gap from that of a beginner to master artist.

Ira Glass shares in a video his lessons learned about the creative process and closing the gap that all creatives face as they learn to get better in their creative field(*I've put a link to the video in the resource section at the end of this chapter*).

I hope Ira Glass's words below inspire you and give you courage to keep writing.

"Nobody tells people who are beginners, and I really really wish somebody had told this to me, is that all of us who do creative work, like y'know we get into it and we get into it because we have good taste, but it's like there's a gap.

That for the first couple years that you're making stuff, what you're making isn't so good, okay? It's not that great. It's trying to be good, it has ambition to be good, but it's not quite that good.

But your taste, the thing that got you into the game, your taste is still killer. And **your taste is good enough that you can tell that what you're making is kind of a *disappointment* to you,** y'know what I mean?

A lot of people never get past that phase. A lot of people at that point they quit. **And the thing I would just like to say to you with all my heart is that most everybody I know who does *interesting creative work*, they went through a phase of years where they had really good taste and they could tell what they were making wasn't as good as they wanted it to be.**

They knew it fell short. It didn't have the *special thing* that we wanted it to have. And **the thing I want to say to you is... everybody goes through that.**

And for you to go through it, if you're going through that right now or if you're just getting out of that phase, *you've gotta know it's totally normal.* And the most important possible thing you could do is do a lot of work.

Do a huge volume of work. Put yourself on a deadline so that every week or every month you know you're going to finish one story.

Because it's only by actually going through a volume of work that you're actually going to catch up and close that gap. And your work you're making will be as good as your ambitions."

In my case, I took longer to figure out how to do this than anybody I've ever met. It takes a while. It's going to take you a while. **It's normal to take awhile. And you just have to fight your way through that."**
~ Ira Glass

Develop Compassion For Yourself as a Beginner

"In his heart, the amateur knows he's hiding. He knows he was meant for better things. He knows he has turned away from his higher nature."

Steven Pressfield, Turning Pro

Developing compassion for yourself and for the beginner writer in you, is that first empowering step you must take toward shifting from a beginner to a master artist.

That compassion is a part of accepting the truth of where you are right now and then giving yourself permission to make mistakes as you learn to write the stories of your heart.

When we first start out as beginning writers, deep inside ourselves most of us know we are scared of venturing out of our comfort zones. Essentially, as new writers we are amateurs that are in hiding.

Deep inside, we really want to write better, to write more and to write for readers who love our stories as much as we do.

But there is still this angsty feeling inside of us that we are waiting for something. Maybe it's validation from someone whom we see as an authority in the publishing world, or maybe it's just permission from family and friends that they would cheer us on in this writing dream of ours.

I can tell you from my own story, that I was waiting for permission from both. I held back on even finishing my first book, not wanting to put it out in the world because I was so unsure of myself. I didn't even know how to name the feeling I had inside or why I was waiting.

Then one day, in the middle of putting off self-publishing my first book, I came across Jeff Goins' book, *You Are a Writer.* My biggest aha moment came when I read his words: *Don't wait for someone to pick you. Pick yourself.*

It was a light bulb moment for me. At last, I realized that all these years of struggling and not finishing my first book, had been about me waiting for permission.

Somewhere in my subconscious mind, I let the negative voices evolve into something much bigger. It dawned on me that I had been waiting for that unknown someone to pick me and validate that I was a writer.

Pick yourself. Let those words sink in and relish their truth.

No big publishing house contract, literary contract or editor needs to confirm what you already know.

You are a writer. Begin to put action to those words.

The day you choose to pick yourself, is a starting point to welcoming the writing gift you've been given with open arms. Take those mind-shifting words to heart and finish your book and keep writing more books after that.

I really hope you will let yourself become what you already are.

You are a writer.
Now it's your turn. Pick yourself.

Letting Go of a Caged Up Writing Life

"Many people live their lives caged either in the past or in the expectations of others. They have never really ventured into the unknown or sought to break the boundaries that they or others have set for them. Because they have let other people or the past dictate who they are, their identities are trapped in a tight box of beliefs about

what is possible for them." Brendon Burchard, *The Charge*

If you can relate to feeling like you are waiting for permission or waiting in some way in fear of the judgment of others, you might be living a caged up life.

If you've waited in fear of others opinions(editors, gatekeepers at publishing houses, people we love, etc) of your writing, you've given your power away even if only in subtle ways.

When we have let others tell us who we are, our identities become trapped in a cage of beliefs about what is possible for us.

This means that our experiences in life and our everyday thoughts, feelings and behaviors are held captive to what others say about us.

Those who are living a caged up life feel shackled to where they are, ruled by experiences they never got over and tethered by the mistakes and failures of the past and scared to disappoint others, especially those whose approval they crave.

I recognize this caged up life, because that was me for years. I let myself constantly be enticed by "carrots" of acceptance and love if my actions fell in line with what was expected of me.

It took choosing to look beyond the walls of my approval and fear-driven experiences to see that there was more to life than being shoved into someone else's cage of what they expected of me. I've been growing in this area to a more authentic, charged up writing life.

If you've been living even parts of your life according

to the expectations of others, I want to encourage you to choose to embrace your authentic self. Choose to do whatever it takes to design your identity so it aligns with what you truly want in your creative life.

Embracing an Authentic Charged Up Writing Life

When you choose to embrace a charged up writing life, you free yourself to believe in more possibilities in yourself and your writing.

If you've been living a caged up writing life, most likely you've been focused on survival and protecting yourself from hurt or pain.

Maybe equally your focus has been about acceptance and belonging.

Wanting to be accepted and to belong are basic universal feelings shared among us as humans.

However, somewhere along the way if we allow our lives to be ruled by our cravings of acceptance and approval, it can balloon into perfectionism or procrastination that cripples our creativity.

I'm well acquainted with perfectionism. It's weighed me down and got in the way of my creativity for years.

Maybe it's done the same for you. In simple terms, perfectionism is this belief that if we try to live, look and act perfect, we can avoid or at the very least lessen the pain of blame, judgement and shame.

Basically, perfectionism is that hundred pound safety shield we carry around in hopes that it will protect us from further pain. At its most basic, perfectionism is about trying to earn approval and acceptance of others.

Dr. Brene Brown in her book, *The Gifts of Imperfection*, shares her thoughts on perfectionism:

> *"Most perfectionists were raised being praised for achievement and performance(grades, manners, rule-following, people-pleasing, appearance, sports).* **Somewhere along the way, we adopt this dangerous and debilitating belief system: I am what I accomplish and how well I accomplish it. Please. Perform. Perfect.** *Healthy striving is self-focused — How can I improve? Perfectionism is other-focused — What will they think?"*

As I read the above statement, what Dr. Brene Brown discovered from her research on perfectionism, it hit me like a ton of bricks.

I had another aha moment: From a young age, I had always tried to perform(in whatever task) to be good enough to win the approval(and acceptance and love) of those close to me.

I realized that this paralyzed me in my writing —in that thing I desired most to do well at — because I was too afraid to put anything out into the world that could be imperfect.

I had a deep fear of failing, making mistakes and disappointing those I loved. I felt like my self-worth(my identity) was on the line every time I tried to write something.

This basically put me in a state of constant paralysis - either hindering or stopping my writing completely.

Needless to say, perfectionism is self-destructive because there is no such thing as perfect. There are flaws in all of us. It's just part of what makes us human.

In my own case, I realized that all this perfectionism had seriously got in the way of my any kind of success in my writing.

It was why I struggled often with depression and anxiety and feeling immobilized for fear of the judgement, shame and rejection that I was convinced would attach itself to me with any writing I put out into the world.

This caused a hamster wheel effect of going around the perfectionism wheel again and running faster and deeper into self-blame. This was the point when I would tell myself: *The reason I feel this way is because it's my fault. I'm not a good enough writer and that's why I'm failing at the very thing I really love and want to be good at.*

These angsty feelings of self-blame and rejection caused me to want to lay low and hide from the world. I didn't want to be seen.

The twin sister of perfectionism showed up. Procrastination.

I continued to be diligent at the small things, but put off really showing up in the world in a larger capacity that I knew was inside me.

In a word, I was hiding.

Tara Mohr, in her insightful book *Playing Big*, shares:

*"There are ways we stall on and talk ourselves out of the very steps that would bring us more fulfillment and enable us to have more positive impact in the world. **All these "hiding strategies" allow us to avoid playing bigger while convincing ourselves we're moving forward in the most diligent way we can**."*

Can you relate to stalling on the very steps you know you need to take?

I've stalled continually on writing projects that trigger fear and insecurity inside me.

I've learned different ways I've used "hiding strategies" to stall and procrastinate on my writing. Maybe one or two of these ideas will resonate with you.

A few ways writers hide so we don't need to put ourselves out there:

• **Making things more difficult than they need to be.** Sometimes we continue to add layers of details to what we need to do, and we end up feeling so overwhelmed by everything that it stops us in our tracks.

For example: "I need to have an author website and email list setup and ready to go before I write my book." The truth is, you don't need to have your website set up first. You could set your website up as you write or get it done when your book is finished.

Many times subconsciously we make things more difficult than they need to be. This includes falling into the trap of doing endless revisions to try to make something really polished(like our writing, or our website design, etc), before we put it out into the world.

• **Setting limits on ourselves by telling ourselves in order to do that, I'll first need to do this.** Sometimes there are things that need to be done before we can do the other thing we really want to do. Many times it's fear that makes us tell ourselves "I just need to do this other thing first" and stops us from taking action and putting ourselves out there.

We come up with stories we tell ourselves, that really are untrue. *For example:* "I wasn't good at writing in school, so I'll need to go back to school to get better at English or get an English Degree before I start to write this book."

The problem is, telling yourself this story is false. There are many bestselling authors who didn't graduate High School like Ray Bradbury, Maya Angelou and Mark Twain. You don't need 'this before that', you just need to begin today.

• **Not sharing your own truth, but trying to make your work abstract or overly complex instead.** Sometimes we create a dividing line between the professional work we do and our personal story. It doesn't have to be this way.

We can acknowledge that we choose work that compels us and share our experiences. *Most of the time the work we are passionate about, is directly related to the core questions we want answers to.*

This way of hiding really resonates with me because

I've struggled to share my story. It's the fear of being vulnerable and being judged that tries to hinders my progress. But I've been learning, even as I write this book, to remove the mask and share why these ideas matter to me.

My encouragement to you is to begin to bravely bare your simple truth as you write. You never know how it will help and transform your life as well as other people's lives.

When we choose to hide instead of sharing our authentic self, we delay fully stepping into a charged writing life.

Stepping out into new levels, stretches us, empowers us and often is the catalyst for change we want to see in ourselves.

Do you best to not be stalled out by fear of being vulnerable and saying what you need to say.

Here's something else I discovered: As I began to accept that I had vulnerabilities and fears of shame, judgement and rejection - and realized that other creatives struggled with the same thing - I began to accept and learn more about who I really was.

This choice, in turn, gave me the courage to practice self-compassion and to forgive myself all my mistakes and flaws.

Self-Compassion as a Daily Practice

"When we become more loving and compassionate with ourselves and we begin to practice shame resilience, we can embrace our imperfections. It is in the process of embracing our imperfections that we find our truest gifts: courage, compassion, and connection." ~ *Dr. Brene Brown, The Gifts of Imperfection*

This is a constant learning and growth process for me. It's a daily practice to tell myself that *you can do this and it doesn't have to be perfect.*

Go ahead and write this whole book imperfectly... it doesn't matter. Simply share the story of your heart.

I find that when I have those kinds of heart-to-heart talks with myself that it frees me up on the inside to embrace the story inside of me that's longing to come out of me and onto the page.

When I've listened to other authors sharing their story on podcast interviews, I've heard them talk about self-doubt or some other kind of resistance they face whenever they sit down to write.

Every writer seems to deal with self-doubt in their own way. To push past their resistance, some writers give themselves a pep talk, some go for a walk, and others find inspiration in books or podcasts.

However, the common theme in dealing with self-doubt, is that successful writers are empowering themselves through valuing themselves and the creativity inside them.

I've noticed that they are choosing to believe they are worthy of their writing dreams. They are choosing to embrace vulnerability and are courageous enough to get to the root of their fears and work through them, giving themselves the grace to learn and grow.

Again, Dr. Brene Brown's research revealed that, *exploring our fears and changing our self-talk are two critical steps in overcoming perfectionism.*

Turns out that deciding to dig deeper into our own fears, no matter how messy, and choosing to speak positively about ourselves, is how we begin to embrace self-compassion and thereby push past perfectionism.

Lessons that I've learned is that speaking about those things we do imperfectly, in a caring and honest way without shame and fear, helps us engage the world from a place of authenticity.

And being slow to judge ourselves and others gives us the courage and compassion to treat ourselves as worthy of our creativity and our writing dreams.

Choosing authenticity and self-compassion, helps us as storytellers to live our own truth and see greater possibilities in our own potential.

In this new place of acceptance of ourselves and our mistakes, we have a new enlarged freedom to begin to Charge Up and Level Up in our writing practice everyday.

Prepare to Upgrade

As writers, when we choose to practice self-kindness and embrace who we really are(mistakes and all), we increase our capacity for creative expression in writing and other areas of our lives.

I've noticed in continuing to practice self-compassion everyday, that my value for myself and my work increases as does my hope and confidence that I can do this writing thing.

As you prepare to upgrade in your writing, embracing self-kindness and authenticity each day as you take steps towards your writing dreams will be a key factor to reaching them.

A Few Simple Steps to Help You Prepare to Upgrade Your Writing:

1.Use creative visualization to design a vision of you and your writing for the future.

Imagine what you really want and make it compelling, exciting and limitless. Think through all the aspects of your writing future.

Write down what you see. Picture yourself working hard on your book and imagine yourself creating a story your readers will love.

Ask yourself if you are writing the story by the seat of your pants or are you writing down story beats or an outline. See yourself writing in time blocks and notice how you are preventing and handling distractions. What does your writing environment look like?

Sometimes it's helpful to observe what one or two of your mentors that have achieved a goal similar to yours and ask yourself what do they do? What's their schedule? How do they market their books?

2. Set the needed buffers in place that will help you overcome obstacles.

Whether you're worried about lack of time, lack of

finances or your ability to create this new writing habit in your life, you need to plan how you will deal with road-blocks on your path.

I encourage you to go back to chapter two, and read through how to push past resistance that tries to block you in reaching your goals.

Also, I encourage you to re-read the start of this chapter to learn how you can practice self-compassion when you make mistakes.

The practice of self-kindness has been so life-changing for me that I believe every writer should learn to do this everyday for themselves. Doing this creates a new freedom to be yourself in your writing.

When you set up buffers in place to deal with what might come up, it'll help your mind relax on those prob-lems instead of worrying.

3. Shift your physical environment and workspace.

Another way to to step into your upgrade in your writing life, is to shift your physical environment.

When you bring your workspace and the physical environment around you to your new level of success you're reaching for, it creates a mainstay for you to hold onto.

For example, I've just cleaned my desk again, and it really inspires me to be more productive in my writing. Somehow creating more space at my writing desk also creates more space mentally.

I encourage you to experiment with changing things around in the space where you write. Sometimes we are so bogged down in how things are, that we can get stuck there.

If you change your environment, then your mind will allow you to shift and become this new creative writer that is in this new space.

This is the new you that has created space for her writing dreams and goals.

Challenges that show up as you prepare to Upgrade

Whenever we choose to level up in any area of our life, it forces us to stretch.

Writing is no different.

It's uncomfortable to shift from where we are currently at, to a new upgraded version of ourselves.

If the upgrade you are making is a simple one that doesn't involve much change, then it won't take much to shift things. But when your plan is to make a massive upgrade in your writing, this will take more planning and effort.

There's a theory that relates to this, called the *rubber band effect*. This effect can be explained by imagining you have a rubber band around you and you can expand the bubble in any direction up to a certain point.

But when you hit a certain point and the rubber band hits its max, it will spring back into place.

You could apply this to any upgrades you make in your writing. If you make changes too quickly you might suddenly revert back to where you were stuck. *For example, if one day you were only writing a 250 words a day and you decide that from now on you'll write 3000 words a day, that's a big jump.* It's possible that you might feel overwhelmed by doing that and you'll fall back to where you first started.

If your current and ideal situation are too far apart, more than likely you'll experience a rubber band effect of stretching until you're maxed out and then snapping back into place.

However, if you begin to shift enough of what you are doing right now in your everyday life to do what it takes to write and finish your book(or books), then you'll start to see for yourself confirmation of change. You'll see that what you're doing is working and that you really can reach your writing goals.

Give yourself permission to move from where you are right now, closer to the state you want to get to, then you'll be able to make the jump to your new upgrade.

3 Problems with Positive Solutions as You Upgrade in Your Writing

1.Making plans to reach your writing goal without learning about possible negatives and positives that you'll experience as you make this shift.

Problem: This is important. Because you are new to shifting to this new level, in your excitement to achieve your goal, you might see everything as rosy, without learning about possible setbacks that might come up.

Solution: Choose to read books, blogposts and listen to podcasts and videos from successful mentors who have gone before you. When you hear their stories of starting out, you'll understand obstacles they went through and how they overcame them. It'll inspire you to do the same.

2.When you start to experience success, it can get too comfortable and you could let yourself slide back to your old way of doing things.

Problem: As you begin to level up and start to see success from your writing, it might be tempting to just relax and go into maintenance mode. If you let yourself do this, it will cause you to lose your momentum, and you'll slide back to where you started.

Solution: Anchor yourself into your new upgrade of regular writing practice and continue to stay steady at learning all aspects of your author business. Staying in this new upgraded space means you need to keep at it.

3.Dreaming of your future success without doing the work.

Problem: Levelling up in our writing takes a lot of work, which most of us don't want to do. We don't want look at all the obstacles and new things we need to learn, so instead we just dream of what we'll do in the future.

Solution: Go ahead and dream of where you want to be in your writing, but then —this is the key point — make an action plan to take that will help you reach your goals. Again learn from successful writers on how they make production schedules and yearly plans.

. . .

It's Your Turn to Charge Up and Level Up in Your Writing

"Before we turn pro, our life is dominated by fear and Resistance. We live in a state of denial. We're denying the voice in our heads. We're denying our calling. We're denying who we really are.

We're fleeing from our fear into an addiction or a shadow career. What changes when we turn pro is we stop fleeing... when we turn pro, we stop running from our fears. We turn around and face them." *Steven Pressfield, Turning Pro*

I've noticed a shift in the mindsets and actions of writer friends who have decided to upgrade their writing practice.

Successful writers have their days, weeks and months ordered with a steady focus on accomplishing their specific writing goals.

Writers who have upgraded in their mindset and practice have chosen to commit to their goals.

They have chosen to structure their days to chase after their writing dreams. They have chosen overcome their fears and do the work.

When we choose deliberate writing practice toward reaching a goal we've set, it completely shifts how and what we do each day. When we're really focused on achieving a goal, it shifts what we do and don't do.

As we choose to upgrade in our writing, this will change who we spend time with and for how long.

As I've been making this shift to level up my writing, I've noticed that people start to see you differently. They'll tell you that you've changed and will try to make you feel guilty for not spending time with them. They might even talk negatively about you behind your back.

But, as sad and hurtful as that is, don't spend time dwelling on it. Instead let it go and focus on the very beneficial changes you are making.

You'll also notice at the same time, there will be other people who are on a similar path as you who are treading down their fears and stepping out to achieve their writing dreams. When you find these inspirational and encouraging friends, that's an incredible blessing. Appreciate them and show them your gratitude.

When you make the shift to level up in your writing, you'll still face the same self-sabotage and resistance everyday. But this time the difference is that you have a new sense of clarity of vision and you've made a decision to do whatever it takes to reach your writing goals.

Many times (if you're anything like me), you've avoided this decision to upgrade for months or years until suddenly circumstances or situations show up in your life to compel you to make a change.

But now you've had your own *aha* moment. It's time for you to finish your book. This is your decision to make a change and level up your writing practice.

You're not alone in making this decision. I've chosen to level up in my writing practice too, as have many other writers I know. I encourage you to find support from other writers.

If you want, you can look for writers groups on Facebook. Just type in your *genre* and the word *writers or authors* in the search bar and see what shows up.

We writers need to stick together and encourage and motivate each other to reach our writing goals.

You can do this. It might take little while to you will do what you must to battle through to get it done.

In the next chapter, I'll share some tips to help you converge into your new normal of living a charged up writing life.

Something to Try...

At the end of each chapter I try offer some simple steps for you to begin to put into practice what you've learned.

I encourage you to take a few minutes to go answer the questions below and to check out the helpful resources.

I believe that going through these exercises, will help bring the clarity and inspiration to finish your book.

Questions to ask yourself:

• Have you hesitated to write your book? Why?

• If you were to relate your writing journey to your school journey, what grade level would you be at? What steps could you take to level up your writing craft?

• Write down a list of 3 things that you feel have held you back from finishing your book.

• What steps can you take to help you develop more self-compassion everyday?

Resources you might find helpful:

• *Turning Pro: Tap Your Inner Power and Create Your Life's Work*, Steven Pressfield

• Blogpost and Ira Glass Video on Closing the Gap between Beginners and Master Artists: www.createasto ryyoulove.com/iraglassvideo

• *The Charge: Activating the 10 Human Drives That Make You Feel Alive*, Brendon Burchard

• Podcast Interview on Stepping Big as a Creative Giant with Charlie Gilkey: https://www.createastoryy oulove.com/charliegilkey

• *Playing Big: Find your voice, your vision and make things happen*, Tara Mohr

• *You Are A Writer (So Start Acting Like One)*, by Jeff Goins

• *The Gifts of Imperfection: Let Go of Who You Think You're Supposed to Be and Embrace Who You Are*, by Brene Brown

• *The Emotion Thesaurus, The Urban Setting Thesaurus and the Rural Setting Thesaurus* by Angela Ackerman and Becca Puglisi.

Chapter Seven

C onverge into Your New Normal

"No masterpiece was shaped or written in a day. It's a long slog to get something right. This knowledge and willingness to iterate is what makes the world's most creative people so creative (and successful)."
Brendon Burchard, The Charge

Now that you have made the decision to level up your writing practice, you might be experiencing some mixed feelings.

The critical voice in your head might be popping up unhelpful comments at you like: *Do you really want to do this, because this is going to take a ton of work.* Or the voice in your head might be saying: *I don't* *like all these changes I'm going to need to make so that I can upgrade. I'm not sure if I can actually do this.*

The creative side of your brain might be saying things like: *Yes, you can write your book and even write and finish more books. You can do what you love and make a good income at it. It's time to finish your book, you can do this!*

If you're hearing both sides, no worries, that's completely normal.

When you come to your breakthrough - if you're feeling what I and many other writers have felt - you will feel exposed as now you see yourself as plain as day.

This is the moment you have an epiphany as you look at yourself in the mirror and say: *Enough is enough, darling. We are not putting up with anymore half-hearted attempts at this writing thing. We are done playing games. Figure out how you're going to take the bull by the horns, write and finish this book and get it out into the world!*

I remember vividly, this defining moment. It was as my husband and I were in the middle of a solid talk(my weird way of saying argument), in which he was sharing his concerns of my slow progress in writing books and that we needed to figure out how to bring more income into our household.

He was totally right, of course. It had taken me such a long time to make any real headway, mostly because I had let fears and insecurities hold me back from writing the stories I wanted to write.

I stood there for a moment as self-delusion was stripped away from me.

Suddenly, I felt this determination rise up on the

inside as I looked him in the eye and boldly said: *I know it's been slow going, but I'm going to change that. I am going to figure this out. I will do this writing thing and make a good income from it, no matter what it takes.*

There is so much power when you arrive at that epiphany moment where you see the naked truth about yourself and your life.

You feel stripped and exposed for what you thought you were doing. You suddenly see the many areas where you've dropped the ball and you feel naked.

The myths you've told yourself for so long must be rejected and you feel the pain of that moment.

But, in all of this angsty self-revelation you are facing, you now see yourself with crystal clear clarity. The scales have peeled away from your eyes and you know without a shadow of a doubt that it's time to make a change.

In the middle of this truth-telling moment, the naked truth humbles you and the reality of your situation is staring you in the face. Both are working in your favor.

This new awareness will catapult you into choosing your next move decisively and strategically.

Which means you are ready to converge into your new normal.

Converge into Your New Normal

Finishing a book and publishing it is exciting. In fact it's downright scary and completely thrilling all at the same time.

Your writing requires creative courage and perseverance.

Being a writer is like a long distance run. When you first start out you feel like sprinting because there's so much to do and so much to learn.

At first, you're excited write the story of your heart but you're also worried because it feels like the stakes are incredibly high. You are excited for people to read your book, but also worried at what they will say.

Then if you choose to write another book(and I really hope you do), you have this mixture of feelings all over again.

Maybe a reader leaves a positive review and you feel like walking on air. Then, maybe a day later a reader leaves a bad review of your book, and you feel like a fraud and want to give up.

This rollercoaster of emotions after you release a book is quite normal. Try to not let the negative comments or reviews of your book get you down.

Stay steady and keep writing. And most of all, don't give up!

Instead, just pause for a moment and let yourself breathe. Reflect on the clear vision and the story ideas that made you excited about writing in the first place.

Remember this isn't a goal that's accomplished in a day or a week, it takes longer than that, with many highs and lows along the way.

Finding a way to manage all the writing angst along with having a life outside of this new and exciting writing path, is vital to sticking with it.

Find time to play with your kids, spend time with

family and take care of yourself mentally and physically in the middle of all the writing.

Writing your book - whether it's your first or your fiftieth - is not easy, but it is worth it.

As you begin to level up in your writing practice, you want to create lasting change.

When you reach this point, you are ready to learn how to integrate into the upgrade you've started.

How to Integrate into Your New Normal

To create any sort of lasting change in everyday life, it means we have to get rid of our old reality.

This is true whether you've decided to go on a new diet, drive a standard car or up your writing game. Each of these choices requires changing past habits so you can shift toward your new normal.

To make this shift, we need to integrate the upgrades we're making in our life and empower ourselves so we develop stick-to-it-iveness in our new normal.

It's especially important to avoid going back to harmful mindsets and habits. But, if you're like me, you will occasionally slide back into old habits.

If or perhaps I should say when that happens, choose self-compassion and then immediately begin to level up again.

Have you ever formed a new habit just to slip back into your old ways?

Maybe you started a walking plan or a new diet and after a few months you stopped being consistent. I know I've done that with daily walks.

I started by being consistent everyday, and then about three months into it, there were a few days here and there where I missed being consistent.

By the time I was five months into it, I had stalled out. I realized something needed to change. For me, when I switched the time of day I walked it helped me be more consistent.

If you have stopped a habit in an area where you were trying to level up, ask yourself what happened and what would help you to be consistent?

Tips to Help You Integrate into Your New Normal

As you start to upgrade in your writing habits, there are a few tips that will help you stay the course and step into a new momentum in your writing practice.

• **Listen to successful mentors and find other writer support:** This is huge. Consistently listening to writers who have started at zero and are now where you want to be will massively increase your confidence.

Learning from and trying advice from mentors will be KEY to help you get out of the old ways of doing things in your writing life(which probably weren't working all that well anyway) so you can experiment with new ideas and upgrade to ideas and methods that work for you.

Some ideas on how you can get the support you need: Read books or blogposts, listen to podcasts or videos, attend a writing conference, join a Facebook group for writers or take an online course from successful mentors who are where you desire to be. As you keep learning, this process will help you to anchor into your goals.

• **Daily Practices of Unblocking, Visualization, Gratitude, Affirmations and Journaling:** Continue to rewire your thinking, so that fears, perfectionism and procrastination lessen and you grow into more self-compassion, confidence and creative freedom in your writing.

Please, look back at chapters two, five and six for tips on how to do this. Choose to take action and visualize your goals and continue to develop self-compassion.

From there your confidence will continue to grow and learn. As you stay steady with your writing, you'll find that taking creative action will bury your fears.

• **Create confirmations in your life that this upgrade is the new you:** It's important to create the evidence you need in your everyday life that you are levelling up in your writing practice.

For example, you could say: "I always write for twenty-five minutes each morning." As you write those words everyday, that will become your new normal and having this confirmation for your writing, will help you stick to your new upgrade.

Then if you miss a day writing you'll be able to tell yourself: *I missed writing for twenty-five minutes today. That's so out of character for me, because normally I write everyday.*

If you are struggling to find the confirmation you need that you are upgrading and accelerating your writing, go ahead and create the evidence you need to affirm that this is indeed the New You!

• **Build systems so around your writing and marketing so you can focus more on what you do well:** When you build a system or a structure around your writing, self-publishing and marketing process, it helps to simplify everything you need to do.

Systems help you get rid of, outsource or simplify what you are doing in your author business, so you can focus more on what you do well.

As you level up your author mindset and business, it's time to take both seriously. This means some of the details you are doing will need to be eliminated, delegated or simplified.

In a podcast interview I had with productivity coach Charlie Gilkey, he shares his thoughts on what it takes to be relentlessly focused and to really level up in your author business(*you can find link to that podcast at the end of this chapter*).

Take an inventory of what you are doing to upgrade your mindset, writing craft, writing momentum, author website and email list, self-publishing, marketing and reader community that are interested in your books.

See what should be eliminated or outsourced and then tweak those things that only you can do, so you can focus and continue to improve on those details.

As you begin to level up to that of a pro writer, you will create the skills needed to help you gain momentum and reach your writing goals.

However, as you go along on your writing journey, you can expect some obstacles to show up to challenge this newfound commitment.

Some Challenges to be Aware of as You Integrate Into Your New Normal

There are some obstacles that will show up on your new pathway to upgrading your writing.

It's inevitable that something will try to hinder your new commitment and it will really help you to be aware of these obstacles so that you can prepare for them ahead of time.

Below is a list of some obstacles that might come up as you begin to integrate and level up in your writing:

• **Your subconscious mind will most likely challenge your newly made commitment to finish your book:** What this means, is that as you write down your vision for your writing and you make it a point to speak out loud your goals and affirmations everyday, your subconscious mind will doubt you.

For example, if you say I am right on schedule to finish this book(insert title of book) by (insert date here) and you've never written a book as quickly as the date you've set for yourself, your subconscious mind won't believe you.

At the beginning, you'll notice that you are definitely not on schedule to finish your book by the deadline you wrote down, but as you keep saying your commitment out loud it will cause you to find the time to write your book and get it finished by the deadline.

Some tips to help you remember to do this: Write this commitment out on a 3 x 5 card or put it on your smartphone where you'll see it everyday and say it out loud before every meal and before you go to bed at night and use an alarm on your smartphone to remind you.

This is a lesson I learned from Honoree Corder in a podcast interview where we talked about the topic of shifting from Hobby Writer to Pro Writer(*You can find the link to that interview at the end of this chapter*).

• **Upgrading too quickly can cause overwhelm:** If you decide you want to go from writing for zero hours to writing for three hours a day, that might be a bit too much and could cause you to feel overwhelmed.

This might leave a bad taste in your mouth about writing which might cause you to procrastinate even more. However, **if you choose instead to begin with smaller writing goals like fifteen minutes or**

twenty-five minutes at a time, this will seem more doable.

By doing smaller timed writing sprints, you will ease into writing and it will become fun for you again and less overwhelming.

• Staying in maintenance mode in your author business might mean you fall behind in your goals: If you decide you want to just get comfortable and stay where you're at as far as writing, self-publishing or marketing your books, it will negatively affect your author business.

The problem with getting comfortable and staying there, is that as an author and as an author business you'll soon discover you're not levelling up and growing.

If you want to write better books and keep in step with this ever growing and changing publishing landscape, you'll need to consistently tweak and change things to build your own author business. *This doesn't need to be overwhelming.*

As you continue to listen to podcasts or YouTube videos by successful indie authors, you'll stay current with what's happening in writing, self-publishing and marketing your books.

I encourage you to read Joanna Penn's helpful book to help you continue to grow as an author called, *How to Make a Living With Your Writing: Books, Blogging and*

More. (I'll add a link in the resources at the end of this chapter).

Of course, there are many other obstacles that will undoubtedly show up, but those mentioned above are some of the biggest roadblocks to achieving our writing goals.

That's why it's so important to uncover ways that work best for you to help you stick with your new writing commitment.

This is where motivation, love of your story and self-compassion come into play. Yes, it's important to be committed to a regular practice of writing and to love what you're writing, but there's something else that really is the foundation for finishing the story we love: *self-compassion.*

I've discovered that when I love the story I'm writing and I give myself permission to make mistakes and to gently ask myself questions to work through issues of procrastination or perfectionism, that's when the answers come and writing becomes much easier.

Maybe to you, it might seem quite 'off-the-beaten-path' to think of self-compassion as a way of motivating yourself to write your book.

I agree it does seem unusual, but please read on. ***I'll explain what I've discovered about choosing self-compassion instead of self-criticism to create the actions you want in your writing journey.***

. . .

A New Way to Motivate Yourself to Finish Your Book

In the past couple of years as I've been learning about how to get out of my own self-imposed writing cage, I've had many epiphany moments.

The biggest epiphany I had was when I began to put into practice Brene Brown's tips in her book *The Gifts of Imperfection*.

I learned that when I act with self-kindness and self-compassion toward myself when I make mistakes, that's when I feel more 'at ease' in my writing process.

This has been an incredible discovery for me. I realized that instead of using self-criticism as a weapon to move me to action to meet my writing goals(which never worked), if I forgave myself for mistakes and found self-compassion as a writer, somehow that gave me a new freedom to write.

With a new freedom to write, I have found that I have wanted to write the books that tugged on my heart - including this one.

When I began to accept myself and my writing, it has changed how I felt. This in turn, has given me a new sense of freedom and space inside myself to embrace the stories of my heart.

I say that not to get all 'woo-woo' on you, but simply to let you know that I've experienced both ends of the spectrum when it comes to writing.

I've experienced the anger, frustration and self-criticism from not meeting my goals in writing and I've also experienced a renewed self-kindness and self-acceptance in spite of all my failures and mistakes as a writer.

I have to say without question, the self-kindness route has been by far, the better choice as it has given me a fresh and love of stories and storytelling and has created an exponential freedom in my creativity and writing.

I want to encourage you, to use motivations that are kinder-to-yourself to reach your writing goals.

Choose self-compassion over self-criticism in all your routines and habits related to your writing practice.

As you choose self-kindness, this will empower you to make the changes you truly desire to happen organically and with a renewed sense of creative flow.

So what are some practical steps to take? Keep reading to learn how you can develop self-compassion as a natural process in your writing life.

Five Ways to Develop Self-Kindness to Let Your Writing Flow

"The essential element in nurturing our creativity lies in nurturing ourselves." ~*Julia Cameron, The Artist's Way*

Since our creativity is nurtured and expanded by our self-compassion, it makes sense to set up habits and routines that would help us to practice this in our writing life.

Here are five ways that have helped me develop self-kindness in my writing practice and have helped take action in my writing:

1.Set 'I want to do this' goals instead of 'I have to do this' goals.

When you set goals that feel joyful to carry out, it's something that you can lean into to help you take action.

Those ideas you are excited to do, typically mirror your unique writing path.

Choosing goals that feel more like self-love have a magnetic pull on you because they express what you truly desire, instead of choosing goals that make you feel burdened, trapped or guilty about something.

There will be some things you do in your writing business that might seem like "I have to do this" goals.

When you find a boring, but essential chore to do(aka like writing out monthly expense and revenue reports for your author business), choose to reframe it to yourself in a way that feels like self-kindness.

For instance, you could look at doing your expense and revenue reports monthly as "I am committed to doing this regularly, so I can create the financial security and peace of mind I really want."

In other words, reframe your *I-have-to* into an expression of *I-want-to* and those mundane tasks will start to feel like you are doing yourself a favor.

. . .

2.Surround Yourself with Encouragers and Accountability Partners.

Part of embracing self-compassion in your writing is to surround yourself with people who will encourage and support you in this new transition and upgrade you have chosen to step into.

When you make an upgrade in your writing, such as finishing your book, it's important to ask yourself who will support and encourage you to help make it easy for you to achieve your goal?

As I've connected with other writers in Facebook groups, I've realized that people who are the most supportive have one thing in common: *they can see the you that is just-emerging and they can see the future that hasn't arrived yet and they tell you that your vision is doable and you are destined to do this.*

I've found this support also in my own husband and children. So look at relationships around you in friends, family, mentors or writing peers that could encourage you in this writing journey.

Besides needing people who support us, we also need those who will hold us accountable to the goals we set for ourselves.

I've found that being accountable to a group of friends in a Facebook Group works well, but find what works the best for you.

Maybe, you have a friend that you could email or call to give you the encouragement and accountability you need to take action in areas where you might be tempted to procrastinate.

In my own experience, I've noticed that when I'm

accountable to someone that I take action, I overcome fears and my behavior shifts to do what I said I would do.

I encourage you to find one or two people who you have as a support and accountability partner to help you make steady progress toward your writing goals.

3. Visualize Yourself in Alignment with a Larger Force

There's third kind of support that you can draw on, which is more spiritual in nature.

See yourself co-creating with a force much larger than you. Some people call this larger force God, the Great Creator, the Universe, or something else.

Whatever you call it, visualize yourself co-creating together with this larger force.

I found that the following quote by Julia Cameron in her book *The Artists' Way,* really resonates in my own writing journey:

"The essential element in nurturing our creativity lies in nurturing ourselves. Through self-nurturance we nurture our inner connection to the Great Creator. Through this connection our creativity will unfold. Paths will appear for us. We need to trust the Great Creator and move out in faith." ~*Julia Cameron, The Artist's Way*

When you see yourself as a co-creator, you will continue to get ideas and inspiration that support you in your writing and this will help you find the motivation to keep writing when you're afraid or stuck.

I've noticed when I see myself as co-creator, I feel empowered and limitless in my creativity and writing.

Ask yourself how different does writing your book feel if you see yourself co-creating with that larger force?

4.Make a Plan Based On Your Own One-Of-A-Kind Strengths and Resources.

You are unique. You as a writer, have whole lot of life experiences and interests, that when they are put together, make up your unique strengths.

This is important to realize as a writer. Because of these one-of-a-kind experiences, passions and strengths that make up you, it means your stories will be different from anyone else's on the planet. That's a wonderful realization to really grab hold of and a great reminder.

What this means is that when you plan what book you're going to write, you'll come at it from a place of your passions and interests with some of your life experiences thrown in.

When you plan your marketing - like the readers you're trying to reach - you'll be focused on reaching readers who are interested in the same passions and interests you write about.

To really narrow down your unique strengths, I encourage you to make a list.

Write down your interests, your passions and your life experiences. Then also make a list of resources you have available to you, including: what skills you're good at, people you know that might be helpful in any area of your writing and access to resources you have available to you.

When you are working to finish your book - be it one book or many - it gives you a rush of confidence and energy when you see the strengths and resources that already exist in your life that could help you.

5. Try Self-Compassion to Search for Answers When You Get Stuck.

As you work on writing and finishing your book, it is inevitable that there will be times when you feel stuck.

Sometimes there will be moments when distraction has caused you to veer off course or there are other details you had to deal with in real life.

However, when you get stuck - whatever the reason - try to search for answers as to why you are stuck, using self-compassion. It's much too easy to beat yourself up and tell yourself you're lazy or a not-so-good writer when you're having a bad day.

Instead of letting your inner critic take over, I want to encourage you to practice self-kindness. This means simply asking yourself: *Darling, what's going on that you are feeling stuck? Why are you letting procrastination slow you down from writing this scene or chapter in your story and what do you need so you can move past it?*

As you listen, the answer will come to you. Simply act on that inner wisdom you hear.

As you begin to use these five ways to develop self-compassion in your writing, I hope it becomes your 'go-to' method to stop self-sabotage and unblock your creativity.

. . .

Next Steps in Your Writing Journey...

The biggest encouragement I want to give you, now that you've finished this book, is to give yourself permission to create the space you need to upgrade your writing practice.

The theme of this book and the seven simple steps to unblock your creativity and accelerate your writing, is something that is a continual growth process.

As you continue to write and finish your book(or books) and stretch yourself in your writing life, you can expect your inner critic to be particularly bothersome. That's normal.

As you follow your calling to finish your book(s), and begin to be empowered in all your communication(writing, blogging, speaking or something else), you can expect that some sort of fear will show up to try to scare you and get you off track. You might even want to retreat back into your comfort zone for awhile.

But I really hope you don't run for cover back to your cave. My hope is that before you retreat back to safety, you will remember to try practicing some of the strategies in this book.

Embrace the changes and the stretching. Accept that mistakes will happen. Choose to step up into new habits.

Some of these changes that will show up in your writing life will be gradual and other changes will seem more sudden.

However, no matter how this shift into your upgrade happens, there's no better feeling than looking around one day with a new awareness of how far you've come.

When you look in the mirror and see that braver version of yourself that has a new freedom to write.

My desire for you now that you've finished this book, is that you embrace the authentic you, and instead of looking for approval from others in your writing that...

• You will follow your own curiosity, your own interests and your own passions.

• You will begin to live with a new creative freedom and joy in expressing your heart onto the page.

• You will converge together a new kind of trust in yourself and the emergence of the story of your heart.

Most of all, I hope that you will be vigilant in your self-compassion so you can push past fears, embrace the wonder and beauty of your story and finish your book.

Something to Try...

At the end of each chapter I try offer some simple steps for you to begin to put into practice what you've learned.

I encourage you to take a few minutes to go answer the questions below and to check out the helpful resources.

I believe that going through these exercises, will help bring the clarity and inspiration to finish your book.

. . .

Questions to ask yourself:

• What unhelpful comments have you heard from the critical voice? How have you replied?

• Have you come to an epiphany where you faced a moment of angsty self-revelation as it relates to your writing? Did you feel a sudden clarity in that moment of your next steps?

• Write down a list of 3 ways that you can choose self-compassion over self-criticism as it relates to your writing practice.

• What steps can you take to help you develop more self-compassion every day?

Resources you might find helpful:

• Tips on building systems around your writing and how to eliminate, delegate and simplify with Charlie Gilkey: https://www.createastoryyoulove.com/charliegilkey

• How to create your own 90 Day Author Plan: https://www.createastoryyoulove.com/90-day-plan

• *Indie Author Mindset: How Changing Your Way of Thinking Can Transform Your Writing Career*, by Adam L. Croft

• Shifting from Hobby Writer to Pro Writer - an interview with Honoree Corder: https://www.createastoryyoulove.com/honoreecorder

• *How to Make a Living With Your Writing: Books, Blogging and More*, by Joanna Penn.

• *The Charge: Activating the 10 Human Drives that Make You Feel Alive* by Brendon Burchard

• *The Gifts of Imperfection: Let Go of Who You Think*

You're Supposed to Be and Embrace Who You Are, by Brene Brown
  • *The Artist's Way,* by Julia Cameron

Are You Ready to Write Your Book?

Join our mailing list and grab your FREE Workbook: *7 Steps to Nail Down Your Novel Before You Start Writing!*
Go here: **https://www.createastoryyoulove. com/storytelling-made-simple-free-pdf/**

Books by Lorna Faith

The Storyteller's Roadmap Series For Writers

Book 1: *Write and Publish Your First Book*

Book 2: *Finish Your Book*

Book 3: *Pre-Order Storytelling Made Simple* Only Available to Pre-Order Direct from my Author Website. **Get a discount on any book when you type in the code: MFB10.** Find out more here: **www.memorablefictionbooks.com.**

Historical Sweet Romantic suspense Series

Book 1: *Answering Annaveta*

Book 2: *Anchoring Annaveta*

Book 3: I need to wait a little while longer before I write the last book in this series. *But it's coming...*

Sweet Bumbleberry Island Clean Romance Series

Dreaming of Love

Grab your FREE Historical Sweet Romance!

Go here: www.lornafaith.com/free-book.

What I'm currently writing(summer 2022)...

Book #1 in a 7 book Middle Grade Fiction series inspired by the true story of my parents and siblings — our family of 13 people — as we pioneered land in the 1960s and 1970s.

A large family struggles to survive the wilderness of Canada's

North battling against unpredictable forces of nature, wild animals and danger to finally forge a clear path in the land and in the growing community and make it a place to call home.

Browse books by Lorna Faith and pen name Melody Archer and get a discount*(use code: MFB10)* **when you buy any book Direct from my Author Website here: https://memorablefictionbooks.com/**

Resources by Chapter

In each chapter I've added a lot of references to books, interviews, videos and articles. I've listed them all here.

If you want, you can download this list at the link below:

www.CreateAStoryYouLove.com/finishy-ourbookdownload

* * *

Chapter One: Clarify Your Reason For Writing

• If you feel you need to re-ignite your passion for writing your story, I encourage you to read the blogpost below: https://www.createastoryyoulove.com/7-ways-to-reignite-your-passion-for-writing/

• How to develop a Practice Mind to go into laser focus with your writing. Interview with Thomas Sterner: www.createastoryyoulove.com/thomassterner

• *Big Magic: Creative Living Beyond Fear* by Elizabeth Gilbert
• *The War of Art: Break Through The Blocks and Win Your Inner Creative Battles* by Steven Pressfield

* * *

Chapter Two: Clear Your Path

• A blogpost of simple steps on how to begin Tiny Habits: https://www.createastoryyoulove.com/tiny-habits
• Dr. B.J Fogg's *Tiny Habits website* on how to start small habits in your life.
• Tips on how to tap into your enthusiasm for your ideas by Mark McGuinness on his website: lateralaction.com.
• *Tips on the pomodoro technique* developed by Franceso Cirillo at francescocirillo.com.
• *Freedom Productivity App* to block the internet
• Podcast Interview with Colleen M. Story on how to unblock your writing path: https://www.createastoryyoulove.com/colleenmstory
• *Story Structure - Demystified* by Larry Brooks.
• *The Hero with a Thousand Faces,* by Joseph Campbell
• Podcast Interview on How to Give Yourself Permission to Create with Pamela Hodges: https://www.createastoryyoulove.com/pamelahodges
• *The Anatomy of Story: 22 Steps to Becoming a Master Storyteller* by John Truby
• *Write Your Novel From the Middle: A New*

Approach for Plotters, Panthers and Everyone in Between by James Scott Bell

- *The Plot Whisperer: Secrets of Story Structure Any Writer Can Master* by Martha Alderson
- Low cost online learning with Udemy.com

* * *

Chapter Three: Calculate Your Strategy

- *Eat That Frog:21 Ways to Stop Procrastinating and Get More Done in Less Time* by Brian Tracy
- Get your Free ebook at the link below: https://www.createastoryyoulove.com/the-storytellers-roadmap
- Video Tutorial on how to write your book using Scrivener: https://www.createastoryyoulove.com/scrivener/
- Video Tutorial on formatting your ebook and print book with Vellum: https://www.createastoryyoulove.com/vellum
- How to setup your wordpress author website video tutorial: https://www.createastoryyoulove.com/video-tutorial-wordpress-website
- *30 Day Author: Develop a Daily Writing Habit and Write Your Book in 30 Days (or Less)* by Kevin Tumlinson
- *How to Market A Book: Third Edition (Books for Writers Book 2)* by Joanna Penn
- Google Keyword Planner Tool to help with keywords for your book
- List of recommended Book Designers: https://www.createastoryyoulove.com/book-cover-design/

• List of recommended Book formatters: https://www.createastoryyoulove.com/formatting

• List of recommended Book Editors: https://www.createastoryyoulove.com/editors

• Learn how to Preview your ebook on Kindle OR how to preview your ePub book here.

• Learn how to create your amazon author page here: https://www.createastoryyoulove.com/amazonauthorcentral

• Learn how to setup your book description on digital retail stores: https://www.createastoryyoulove.com/bookdescriptiongenerator.

• Blogpost on thebookdesigner.com on how to use KDP Print: https://www.createastoryyoulove.com/createspaceandkdpprint

* * *

Chapter Four: Commit to the Writing Process

• *The Anti-Procrastination Mindset: The Simple Art of Finishing What You Start* by Harry Heijligers

• *The Miracle Morning for Writers: How to Build a Morning Ritual that Increases Your Impact and Your Income* by Hal Elrod, Steve Scott and Honoree Corder.

• Heinlein's 5 Simple Rules for Writers: https://www.createastoryyoulove.com/heinleinsrules

• How to Start Simple Habits to Reach Your Writing Goals with bestselling NonFiction author Steve Scott: https://www.createastoryyoulove.com/stevescott

• *The Artist's Way* by Julia Cameron

• *Walking in this World* by Julia Cameron

* * *

Chapter Five: Concentrate on Reaching Your Goals

• *Willpower: Rediscovering the Greatest Human Strength* by Dr. Roy F. Baumeister and John Tierney

• Article and Video on How the Mind Works and how it relates to Intention through to Initiative by prolific coach, Brendon Burchard - https://www.createastoryyoulove.com/brendonburchard

• Article on Jerry Seinfeld's Chain Method as told by Brad Isaac: www.lifehacker.com/jerryseinfeld

• *2K to 10K: Writing Faster, Writing Better, and Writing More of What You Love* by Rachel Aaron

• *You Are A Writer (So Start Acting Like One)* by Jeff Goins

• *On Writing: A Memoir of the Craft* by Stephen King

• *Write Down the Bones* by Natalie Goldberg

• *Deep Work: Rules for Focused Success in a Distracted World* by Cal Newport

• *Creativity: Flow and the Psychology of Discovery and Invention* by Mihaly Csikszentmihalyi

• How you can learn to trust story emergence – an interview with NY Times bestselling author Joanna Penn: www.createastoryyoulove.com/joannapenn

* * *

Chapter Six: Charge Up and Level Up

• *Turning Pro: Tap Your Inner Power and Create Your Life's Work*, Steven Pressfield

• Blogpost and Ira Glass Video on Closing the Gap between Beginners and Master Artists: www.createasto ryyoulove.com/iraglassvideo

• *The Charge: Activating the 10 Human Drives That Make You Feel Alive,* Brendon Burchard

• Podcast Interview on Stepping Big as a Creative Giant with Charlie Gilkey: https://www.createastoryy oulove.com/charliegilkey

• *Playing Big: Find your voice, your vision and make things happen,* Tara Mohr

• *You Are A Writer (So Start Acting Like One),* by Jeff Goins

• *The Gifts of Imperfection: Let Go of Who You Think You're Supposed to Be and Embrace Who You Are,* by Brene Brown

• *The Emotion Thesaurus, The Urban Setting Thesaurus and the Rural Setting Thesaurus* by Angela Ackerman and Becca Puglisi.

* * *

Chapter Seven: Converge Into Your New Normal

• Tips on building systems around your writing and how to eliminate, delegate and simplify with Charlie Gilkey: https://www.createastoryyoulove.com/ charliegilkey

• How to create your own 90 Day Author Plan: https://www.createastoryyoulove.com/90-day-plan

• *Indie Author Mindset: How Changing Your Way of*

Thinking Can Transform Your Writing Career, by Adam L. Croft

• Shifting from Hobby Writer to Pro Writer - an interview with Honoree Corder: https://www.createastoryyoulove.com/honoreecorder

• *How to Make a Living With Your Writing: Books, Blogging and More,* by Joanna Penn.

• *The Charge: Activating the 10 Human Drives that Make You Feel Alive* by Brendon Burchard

• *The Gifts of Imperfection: Let Go of Who You Think You're Supposed to Be and Embrace Who You Are,* by Brene Brown

• *The Artist's Way,* by Julia Cameron

About the Author

Lorna Faith is an author of historical romance and other books she has in different stages of writing.

As if this writing, she is enjoying writing a new middle grade fiction series inspired by true events from her childhood.

Lorna has a growing website, focused on helping writers to get their books into the world.

Check out this new Video and Blogpost series: *7 Steps to Nail Down Your Story Idea Before You Begin Writing.*

Grab Your Free PDF Workbook here: https://www.createastoryyoulove.com/part-1-brainstorm-story-ideas

Lorna's website for writers is dedicated to helping first-time writers, to write, self-publish and market their books.

Through many blogposts, podcasts and videos, Lorna shares what she has learned and continues to learn in hopes that it will help others to write the stories they love.

Lorna has a Bachelor of Music Degree from the University of Lethbridge, Alberta. When she's not busy teaching piano lessons she's scribbling on a new book.

Besides enjoying adventures with her husband and four young adults, she dreams of travelling someday and soaking up even more historical inspiration, amazing architecture and exotic foods.

Lorna's happy place is writing more stories and helping writers get their stories into the world!

Connect with Lorna by clicking on your favorite social media links below!

facebook.com/createastoryyoulove

instagram.com/createastoryyoulove

pinterest.com/createastoryyou

Acknowledgments

Thank you to Heather Cole for editing this book... I am grateful for your patience and all your hard work!

This book is dedicated to all those successful authors who have taken time and resources to help other struggling authors just like me.

Thank you for your dedication as you take the time to help the rest of us write our stories. :)

Thank you to the readers and writers who connect with me at CreateAStoryYouLove.com.

Your encouragement and support inspires me to continue this storytelling and author entrepreneur journey.

Thanks to the readers of the blog and newsletter who helped me by doing a survey and who have been patiently waiting for this book. I appreciate you all!

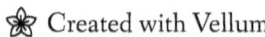